# Part One

# Chapter 1

I was a new reporter, still three weeks away from actually starting work, and the biggest story in Europe was on my doorstep. I watched boys building a barricade at the end of our street in the Riverdale estate. I watched the local IRA elders supply those boys with crates of petrol bombs, and then depart. The usual definer of difference between young men and older men was responsibility. It didn't apply here. Adults were as excited as children. The elders supplied the logistical support. My place in all this excitement would soon be to report it. I was eager to start; I feared the escalation was leaving me behind.

Political violence had been growing for three years and would now take off more sharply. This was 9 August 1971. The British army had just raided hundreds of houses and arrested 300 men, all of them Catholics suspected of being members of one or other faction of the IRA. The government of Northern Ireland at Stormont ordered the arrest of hundreds of suspected insurgents and their internment without trial.

Journalism comes late when the streets are already on fire. We could see the columns of smoke around the city. We could hear the distant and sporadic rattle of gunfire. The morning paper, if it had got to us, would have been no use. People believed rumours and passed them on. So women came to our door to tell us that 'they' were going buck mad up in Moyard. They were. And that the cathedral down the road was in flames. It wasn't.

I was at home alone with my sister Bríd. My mum and dad were on holiday in Donegal with my youngest brother Niall. Brian, closer in age to me, was working the summer in England, well out of it. My older sister, Anne, no longer lived at home. My twin brother, Roger, was the politically astute one. The night before, we had speculated on when the army would move to intern suspects. We tried to think like their advisors. This was a boys' game too but we guessed right. A loyalist parade planned for Thursday in Derry would have to be banned. The government, to win the moral authority to ban it, would move against the IRA first. The earlier, the better. Having made his calculation, Roger left the house and urged me to do the same. When the army swept, it might lift every young man of martial age, however little martial inclination he might actually have.

The boys at the end of the street were just waiting for something to happen, like a football team waiting for the ball. A delivery van pulled up behind them and two of my neighbours climbed out and unloaded crates of petrol bombs through the back door. These were men who had chased me from the front of their houses as a wild boy when I was making too much noise, frightening their children or jeopardising their windows. Now they were more eager for chaos than I had ever been.

Why was I not with the boys on the street, getting ready for a rattle at the army? Because you could get killed doing that. And I didn't even know most of them. They were peripatetic rioters from Lenadoon and Whiterock and other estates. Would they even have accepted me if I had wanted to join them? I felt as if I was standing at the side of the pitch. Did I want to join them? No; they fascinated me but they appalled me too. I was suspicious, though, of my own good sense in not wanting to be part of this, because it was laced with fear. Would I have been more eager to join this revolt on the streets if I had believed in their cause and thought this was a realistic way to pursue it, which I didn't? No; I knew then too that even if I had agreed with the boys on the street, and with the neighbours who sheltered and supplied them, I would have found it difficult to take part. A street fighter needed something other than conviction. He needed to enjoy the danger and the damage.

However, it wasn't feasible to respond as if this wasn't happening. So, journalism would be my place in the game. It would suit my need to be part of the adventure of chaos without my having to be brutal or to accept anyone's orders. Journalism would satisfy my detachment from the raw charge of enthusiasm for war which had overtaken so many people around me.

I was alone in the house with Bríd. She was just a year older than me. Her boyfriend was a Protestant and a policeman. There would be little chance of reaching him, little sense in him coming to us.

I walked over to the barricade. It was a flimsy erection of crates and planks, designed not to deter soldiers but to attract them. Tommy Gorman and some of the other boys were there, their shirt sleeves rolled up for fighting. I don't know what they made of me. To them, it must have seemed strange that a young man of 20, like themselves, was staying out of this. But they were part of something together, with a command structure and a plan. I suspect I was invisible to them.

Just then, a solitary army Land-Rover came up Finaghy Road North and stopped near the motorway bridge. I assumed at first that the soldiers would try to clear the barricade. So, there would be trouble, as the boys had expected. I turned and walked briskly back to the house, knowing how dangerous this was. The boys, knowing as clearly too, mustered their stones and petrol bombs and ran to the corner to pelt the soldiers. There were two loud bangs: the soldiers firing rubber bullets. The sound was fuller and darker than the crack from a gun would be. The rubber bullets were black and hard and about the size of a large shampoo bottle, designed to bounce between rioters and bruise their legs, unless fired straight at their heads, which they often were. I got to the house. I was breathless.

'Get inside.'

Bríd was frantic, grasping at me with her eyes, as if I might have some answer. I hadn't. There were frightened younger boys running through our garden and round to the back of the house. I opened the living-room window and yelled at them to clear off. They would draw the soldiers in our direction. Then I wondered if I had betrayed myself to them as someone who didn't care if they got shot so long as I didn't get shot myself. We then heard two loud cracks of rifle fire. That's when it became serious. I began to imagine bullets cracking the brickwork, smashing through the windows. We were defenceless. Bríd and I turned to each other helplessly. We crouched as if for prayer and, when that felt just as stupid as lying down would, we lay down. And waited. The soldiers might come around the corner and keep shooting up the street or they might hold their ground and wait for support. The IRA might return fire and prolong a battle. That's what they were doing in other areas.

But that was it. There was no more shooting.

The boys started crossing the garden again back to the street to see what had happened. The soldiers had simply shot someone and left. Why had they stopped then? What did they want that was worth shooting their way through for? Had they retreated to return with more force later?

I went out to the front of the house. Death had come to

the street but the atmosphere had not changed. It was a lovely summer's day. My neighbours on both sides of the street were standing around dazed. The word was that the soldiers had shot Frank McGuinness. Bríd had his name before I had. I had known Frank McGuinness and his brother a few years earlier. Bríd was getting the gossip. She heard that he had not been one of the rioters. He had not run because he wasn't doing anything wrong, people said. Someone described how, when the men had tried to lift him into a car, a large slab of coagulating blood had flopped like a burst ball onto the road.

I had to get busy. Today, after years of experience, I would know what to do as a journalist in a crisis like that. To think back now and see myself so helpless there is embarrassing. The newspaper that I would start work on in a couple of weeks was *The Sunday News*. The daily paper from the same office, *The News Letter*, was pro-government and would, I suspected, be unsympathetic. Besides, the little incident in front of our house was one of many like it that day. I phoned a reporter at *The News Letter*. I said, 'The soldiers shot an unarmed boy. His name is Frank McGuinness.'

The reporter said, 'I'm sure they did.'

I hadn't seen the angle that made the incident newsworthy, which, on reflection, was simply that the soldiers had not been part of a raiding party making arrests; that they could simply have driven past and avoided trouble but had found irresistible the opportunity to kill someone.

Many years later, Tommy Gorman, one of the IRA men who led that riot, told me that Frank McGuinness had been throwing stones at the soldiers.

> When Frank was shot, I was standing pretty close to him. There was this thing in below his arm and I said, 'He's only wounded.' There was a long wound and I thought it had just skimmed or took the flesh, but apparently the bullet went in

and rattled about inside. He would have been dead very quickly.

Martin McLaughlin saw it too. He had been walking near his own home on Finaghy Road North.

> It wasn't a riot really. An army vehicle came up the road and a few young lads started chucking things at it. I saw one of the soldiers get down on one knee and shoot a boy from about a hundred yards. It was horrific. Then they just got back in the vehicle and drove off.

That night, my mother and father came back from Donegal. They had enjoyed their journey to rescue us from the front line and take us back with them. I slept that night at a neighbour's house. The sensible thing was for young men not to sleep at home. The next morning, we headed off northwest to the border.

I should have been going into town to sign on the dole but I was confident the desk clerk would understand. In fact, he wouldn't and when I would write 'bombs and bullets' on my excuse slip a week later, he would give it back to me and ask me to write a 'proper' reason. I would then write that I had been ill.

The only other signs of trouble were in Derry, 75 miles away. It was easy to imagine from Derry or Belfast that the whole region had plunged into war but that day you could have had a picnic on any beach, walked on any mountain and seen perhaps only a distant wisp of smoke that might as easily have been a farmer burning weeds as a row of houses under attack.

Donegal was distant from the trouble in Belfast, but interested in it. I didn't like those people who had no involvement but would exercise their passions on it and even influence its progress. Or, to put it more plainly, when I heard a man in a bar sounding off about the British occupation or the need to send the Protestant planters back to Scotland, I usually voiced the words, if only in my head: 'What do you know about anything?'

My father, Barney, had deeper roots in this Donegal culture than in the republicanism of Belfast. For him, the eruption had been historically inevitable, part of a story he thought he was already familiar with. My generation, which ironically included most of the new IRA members, was, in his view, ill-placed to speak on what was happening, and certainly, as far as I was concerned, ill-placed to criticise.

Barney had been a republican in his thinking, without reservation, since childhood. The illegal British occupation of a part of Ireland was simply a fact of life for him, like the Second World War or the passage of the seasons. The partition of Ireland to preserve a Protestant state was just plain wrong and that state would have to be reunited with the rest of Ireland in time, regardless of the will of the majority there. He had probably never felt the need to take seriously anyone who disputed that. As for the Protestant people themselves who opposed this: well, they had no right to oppose it.

'They are taught to hate us. Well, they can't have their way. That's that. What do they know about anything?'

When the shooting started in August 1969, my father managed two bars owned by a Catholic family in a Protestant area. On the morning of 15 August, I had visited one of the bars and noticed the colder attitude of customers who had previously been friendly. We closed the bars early. That night, Protestant rioters burnt them to the ground. Next day, my brother Brian rummaged in the rubble for the cash box.

'They turn on you,' Barney said.

One night, during that week in Donegal, we drove to Milford for a political meeting. The hall in the Milford Inn was dark and crowded to the back wall with people from the surrounding area. These were the locals, not the tourists. My father would have regarded himself as one of them. I was a tourist. It suited my outsider status to imagine myself a reporter. Had I been in my job, this was a story the paper would have appreciated. The two speakers were members of the Dáil (the Irish parliament), Kevin Boland and Neil Blaney. Both had strong ideological republican convictions. Both were critical of their party leadership's qualified support for nationalists in the North. Blaney looked a bit like Barney. He had a similarly lined face — textured almost like wood — and a rounded balding crown. Barney told us that Blaney was a distant cousin, too distant perhaps to allow him to approach him, though we would surely have been received as heroes, refugees from the war zone.

'Today,' said Boland, 'I had the unusual experience of driving north into the North and further north back into the South.' The crowd appreciated the joke as if geography itself refuted the hated border. Northern Ireland was frequently called Ulster. 'Last time I looked at the map, there were nine counties in Ulster, three of them on our side of the border.'

Simplistic politics fed this intense nationalistic ardour. I said nothing because I was sick of arguing with Barney, but he was on a kind of high that night. Having driven in silence through the dark and narrow mountain roads back to Port Salon, he said quietly, like an unconscious leakage from his intense deliberations, 'Cometh the hour, cometh the man.' He was overtaken by sentimentality about the historic importance of those days and by a sense that heroic and historic challenges were ahead of us.

My mother was not a republican and I have tended more to her views than to my father's. When she saw me reading her own father's copy of Dan Breen's *My Fight for Irish Freedom*, she sneered at Breen and called him a brute. She had a hierarchy of patriots in her mind. When she was six years old, her own mother had slumped over the kitchen table in tears at the news that Michael Collins was dead. I could have argued with her that Collins and Breen had served the same cause in the same way, yet to her Collins was a soldier and ultimately a peacemaker, while Breen was a lout like Tommy Gorman and the other boys on the street.

Mum had nursed in London during the war and seen bombings that made Belfast's worst look insignificant. There is a story circulating in the family that she had had a soldier boyfriend, a paratrooper who had died at Arnhem, but the story is constructed from unfinished sentences muttered under sudden unexpected tears, quickly dried. She was in her thirties before she married my father after the war, so she must have had many friends and experiences of which we know nothing.

Mum was enjoying that summer. The only quarrel she and Dad had on that Donegal trip was over her kissing a man in a bar. I was there; it was just a flirt, a quick peck. The man was half her age and obviously just playing. It seemed ridiculous to me that my father would fret about it for hours, but he did. Perhaps he was still just fretting about her war years. I think that was the last time I saw her playful. She was 55 years old, the age I am now. She was on holiday and merrily, not darkly, drunk. She was relieved of a heavy work routine; that was part of it. Maybe she was happy that she had enlarged the holiday party in the rented cottage with us refugees from Belfast and maybe — like others — she was a little elated by the violence and change. We might not know what was going to happen but we knew that something was. This I doubt, though. The troubles had been horribly demoralising for her and I had already seen her at times so fraught that she was almost shrieking in ordinary conversation.

# Chapter 2

I put on a tie for my first day at work. I wouldn't need one after that. I took the familiar bus route down the Falls Road. This was the road into the centre of Belfast that I knew best. It was also the road that had suffered the most rioting. From my seat on the upper deck, I could see bullet marks on the walls, the sworls of melted tarmac where cars had been burnt on barricades, and the ruins of buildings. This road was Catholic and nationalist. It ran roughly parallel to the Shankill Road which was Protestant and unionist. Soon after the British army came into Belfast in August 1969 to impose order on rioting mobs, they had built a wall to divide the Shankill from the Falls, splitting the connecting streets, first using barbed-wire coils, then corrugated iron. Later, the walls would grow longer and higher and be built of bricks to keep the people of Protestant and Catholic neighbourhoods apart, for their own safety.

The centre of town was neither Catholic nor Protestant. The rioting gangs had not assembled there, and people moved in relative safety from them, if not from the bomb attacks on shops and offices. For over a year now, republican and loyalist groups had been delivering bombs to bars and other businesses, occasionally killing small numbers, usually giving warnings of a few minutes to half an hour, for managers and shop girls and grey-haired security men to clear customers.

The newspaper office was in Donegall Street, beside St Anne's Cathedral, a huge grey-stone block which a dean has since ordered scrubbed of a century of city pollution. Donegall Street was not named after County Donegal, to the northwest of us in the South, but after an aristocrat who had taken the name and retained a different spelling. I had rarely been down this street and I was nervous, but more nervous of meeting the people I would work with, and the challenge of finding a place among them, than of the physical danger.

Something was going on already. There were about a hundred people standing on the footpath outside the cathedral. A crowd like this was usually the evacuated staff of some office building that had received a bomb alert. I was shy of asking any of the people which building they had come from and walked straight through them to the front door of Century Newspapers and inside to the vacant reception area. I should have worked it out by now. I stood and looked around me and did not know what to do, hampered by teenage self-consciousness from running back out. I wonder how many people lose their lives working to retain composure, trying not to look foolish, stopping to get dressed as a fire engulfs a stairwell or an earthquake shakes the walls. Maybe the receptionist was at the toilet and would be back in a minute. Maybe. More likely she was with the evacuees outside, wondering if she would ever see her typewriter or filing cabinet again.

The door opened again behind me.

'Come on, sonny; it's a bomb scare.'

There were always more hoaxes than actual bombings, so people usually assumed that they were in no real danger. A few soldiers would search the building, perhaps with a dog, and declare after half an hour that there was nothing there, even though they couldn't possibly have looked in every drawer or feasible hiding place. Belfast people were relaxed even about evacuation because they were coming to know the rituals and methods of those who threatened them and that bomb threats phoned in to an office were usually jokes in poor taste. It was the bombs carried in and set on the counter in front of you that you had to believe in. Soon there would also be bombs in cars parked outside.

I followed the man back to the crowd. Briskly. And then I stood apart, not knowing anyone, waiting for the all-clear. I was standing with people I felt I would not be at ease among. They were good-humoured. They were middle class. Fat men of 50 in shirts and braces joked with office girls in miniskirts about how quickly they would be able to run, in high-heeled shoes, from a real bomb. They were more neatly and expensively dressed than I was and more easily affable with each other. And their humour centred on an unabashed contempt for the bombers and hoax-callers. I lived among bombers and heard little criticism of them at home or from my neighbours. I had ambiguous feelings about them. I was morally confident that they were wrong in their methods; but I could not heartily share in a mockery of their political rationale. And those who were unionist and Protestant, who were confident in their history and position, made no distinction between ideas and method when sneering at those who brought bombs into their workplaces. And a moment at which they were under threat seemed a tactless time to correct them. Therefore I immediately felt shamed into silence. That sense of shamed silence would stay with me all the time I worked at the newspaper.

Someone shouted out: 'We're spared today!' And the crowd, laughing and joking, turned towards the office building and went back to work. The chatty woman at reception, who seemed all the more alien for knowing everyone but me by first name, asked me to wait and she summoned a reporter to take me through narrow corridors and several levels to the office of *The Sunday News*. There, a cluster of men gathered with no sense of urgency around an island of desks, piled with papers and phones that were tangled together under the gaze of a naked woman on a poster that filled one whole wall. Was this what the world of work looked like? I had expected it at least to look busy.

It was like joining a group of workmen, standing round a hole, thinking about whether or not to fill it in, but in no hurry.

Another reporter was starting work on the paper on the same day as I was. Eddie was my own age but already had two years of experience on a provincial paper.

'Hello,' he said. 'First job?'

Eddie was a silent and tidy man with a gentle sense of humour. There was nothing bawdy or extravagant in his manner, though there often is among journalists. He struck me immediately as shy, but no reporter is shy. So he combined a modest reserve with the ability to talk to people. He came across as if he was already a bit wise to pretension and brashness. I had plenty of both with which to impress him. Any journalist will look through human nature, and even human suffering, with the detachment of a surgeon, accustomed to feints and follies. Eddie would not be fooled, or at least he conveyed a confidence that he would make a balanced assessment of people, but he did not swagger. He was a Protestant, but that says nothing very important about him, unless you think, as many do, that there are Protestant manners and attitudes. My mother used to joke, after combing my hair when I was a little boy: 'There now, that's a bit more Protestant-looking.'

It meant too, of course, that he probably went home to a neighbourhood which was rarely if ever raided by the army, which was not barricaded — yet — and that his sleep was broken only by distant gunfire and explosions. I might be wrong about that.

Another reporter, Rick, joined us a week later. He too would have fitted some of my stereotypes of the Protestant. He was stiff and formal, dealt with issues in a reasoned and dispassionate way, never argued and never betrayed any contempt for people on sectarian grounds. He had a habit of sniffing at what you said to him, as if he was actually tasting your words for traces of good sense and logic, but with little expectation of finding any.

As a journalist, he naturally mocked all politicians in conversation but showed no favour that I could detect. Once when we were talking about internment, which I opposed on moral or human rights grounds, he explained to me his own pragmatic objection: 'It makes it impossible for moderate nationalists in the SDLP to support the government policy. That screws up any chance of winning Catholics into a strategy against the IRA. That's why it's a bad idea.'

I was impressed by Rick's practical reasoning and wondered if he thought I was being childish in responding to political questions in the same terms as any of my neighbours. His take also impressed me as individual rather than as a party position. I had assumed that most Protestants cared little for any nationalist political co-operation.

There was Paddy, a big hippy. He had long red hair and a red beard.

'Don't pay any attention to what anyone says to you. Me neither.' Paddy was outside the simple stereotypes too. He was cryptic at times but probably the most intelligent of us all. I doubt if Paddy had any strong affiliations in the Northern Irish sense. Sometimes people like him are regarded as weak and unprincipled or as apologetic, reviled for not meeting the communal, political or religious expectations of others. Paddy was not under any onus to conform, yet he did, in a sense, belong to a category — of people who had grown up in Northern Ireland in secular or socialist homes, who were perceived by others as Protestant because they were not Catholic, and for whom the great question of whether they were Irish or British was simply tiresome and irrelevant. Many of these people perhaps tilted more towards being Irish, but more to show Catholics that they felt no animosity towards them than because they really wanted to be governed from Dublin. Paddy had had a liberal education in a cosmopolitan family and was unpredictable in his opinions, at least to a callow youth like me.

Jim was the news editor.

'Right! Let's see some work done.'

His desk was set back from the island, in a corner, under the naked-woman poster. He was brash and voluble. He told stories about his own time in the IRA in his teens. He had no fear of anyone in the office knowing that he had been in the IRA. At first, his stories astonished me. After a time, I began to doubt them. They were just too neat and marvellous.

Later, we would be joined by Stephen, a Canadian.

'What is it about this fucking country?'

Together we would work in a light-hearted office, divided, when divided at all, by moods rather than by questions. If anyone was sectarian there, it was me, the one who had had least exposure to life outside the streets he had grown up in, the one who most assumed that the political positions held by his peers were right and good and that those of all others, particularly Protestants, were narrow and vicious.

Jim didn't like me at first. He was determined to humble my pretensions to be a real journalist before he would teach me the job. In my own mind, I was now a proud professional with a salary, the most unlikely thing to be. I wondered if someone had made a mistake and allocated me to an absurdly elevated role in life, for no good reason other than that I had been rash enough to ask. But the first question was whether or not I could really do this job. It was a kind of consolation that the paper was regarded as superficial and sensationalist. I could do superficial and sensational — second nature to me really.

Jim's first assignment for me was beyond my skills and he knew it. He wanted me to conduct a big investigation into an international hotel chain. The story was that the chain was bringing in foreign girls, holding their passports, providing them with cheap accommodation and paying them low wages. So they came to Belfast and had no life outside their work and no prospect of moving on to other jobs. I was to look into it.

I went into the hotel lounge feeling like Sam Spade, sat at the little mirror-fronted cocktail bar and helped myself to a fistful of salted peanuts from a crystal bowl. A barman in a crisp white shirt and black satin waistcoat was polishing glasses. 'Can I help you, sir?'

Nobody had ever called me 'sir' before.

As he poured me a long beer with a head you could have washed your hair in, I asked him if he liked the hotel business. He did. This was a good company to work for, he said. Were there many foreign workers here? No problem with that. Were they happy? It seemed so to him.

Then what? Then I didn't really know where to take this without declaring that I was a reporter.

Jim's source for the story had a phone number for a house where many of the girls were staying. Sam Spade would have hung around outside, taken one of the girls for a ride in his car, pumped her for info and then made love to her in the back seat. I didn't feel up to that. I phoned the number. I said I was a journalist. I said if any of the girls weren't happy with their conditions, I would do a story. I left the office number with them. Next day, a girl called the office and asked for me. She hung up when I took the phone. Then the press officer for the hotel group phoned and asked to see me. He gave me a tour of the kitchens to see that they were clean. 'I never doubted it,' I said.

I worked out that this would be a humiliating job if Jim just handed me stories to do and I failed to complete them. Some days, I sat at my desk and he gave me nothing to do all day. It was as if he were waiting for me to act on my own initiative. But how?

One evening, I went for a walk up through the grounds of Belfast Castle with my friends Maguire and Fegan. In troubled Belfast, we often found ourselves doing aimless things like that. The killing of random Catholics had started but wasn't yet so routine that we would be afraid to walk through dark woods. We talked mostly about what sort of future we would find away from there. Fegan had decided to go to Dublin. He had family in the city who would put him up. Maguire was our philosopher. He just had a cold way of looking at things and he never disclosed much in the way of ambition. He had been away and come back. It was Maguire who noticed that there was a light on in the castle, on the top floor. 'I bet they'd shite themselves if we knocked the door.'

Next day, I phoned the Parks Department and they told me that a caretaker and his family had an apartment inside the castle. Otherwise, the entire building was unused. It was very beautiful inside, they said. This would be my story: the family that lives in a castle. It would make a perfect photo feature — the children sliding down the banisters of the sweeping staircase. So I phoned the family and spoke to the woman and she said no; they didn't want to draw attention to themselves at these difficult times. I had seen how Jim bullied and cajoled people into giving way to him, so I locked into exactly the same manner.

'You know we can do this story anyway. But if you co-operate, you have some influence over how it turns out.'

Jim was aghast.

'Malachi, it is not an important story. It is not an exposé. If you want to talk to people like that, go back round to the hotel; talk to *them* like that.'

# Chapter 3

I moved between two worlds now. At home, I lived with my parents, brothers and sisters, coping with fearful change around us. The IRA had moved into our street. Just two days before I started work on *The Sunday News*, one of the local gunmen had shot Clifford Loring, an 18-year-old soldier in the Royal Artillery Regiment. The bullet that hit him had passed through another soldier's flak jacket first. Clifford died the day I started work.

It was also in my first week there that an IRA gunman shot and killed baby Angela Gallagher off the Falls Road. A shot fired from a car had ricocheted. The gunman could not have seen the children. The IRA said it was the sort of thing that happened in a war. They were right; it was. Inevitably, with so much daytime shooting in residential areas, bullets would fly astray into the wrong bodies. Angela's seven-year-old sister said later that she had heard a loud bang, then something passed between her knees and made a hole in her dress. Wee Angela fell out of her pram. She couldn't lift her.

The front-page picture in most of the daily papers showed Angela's father carrying the coffin in his two hands at the head of the huge funeral. We, as a weekly paper, didn't have to go out and cover these killings.

Later in the week, the Official IRA blew up John Warnock, a soldier from Wiltshire. John was 18 and married. In Derry, on the same day, a bullet crashed into the frail body of a 14-year-old girl, Annette McGavigan. She had blithely walked into crossfire between the army and the IRA to try and pick up a rubber bullet for her collection of riot souvenirs. Annette was the hundredth civilian to die and the fourth aged 18 or under to be killed that week.

In the office of *The Sunday News*, we would sit down every Tuesday to think of stories for the paper. I could have got stories about a local IRA unit, E Company, led by Sean Convery and made up of Tucker Kane, Tommy Gorman, Jim Bryson, Tommy Toland, Eddie Carmichael and others. I could have written about those gunmen themselves. I watched them standing guard with weapons, retrieving their guns from dumps in the gardens and sniping at army patrols on the main roads. I could have written about the takeover of streets by the paramilitaries, about the women who provided them with safe houses or billets. I could have written about the strain of living in such a street, uninvolved in the new angry culture. I wrote about none of these things.

There were then about 45 newspapers published in Northern Ireland every week. Sectarian division was good for the newspaper industry. Every largish town and county capital had two papers, a Protestant paper and a Catholic paper. We scanned these papers for stories that we could pick up for our own pages. Sometimes we would simply rewrite a story, but occasionally we would look further into it, follow it up, and go out with a photographer for our own pictures. A farmer in County Fermanagh was trapping otters in a river. A woman in County Down had set up her own boutique to sell clothes she designed and made herself.

I showed a bit of initiative by trawling the ads too. One day, I noticed an appeal for people to look out for a lost cat.

His name was Sasha. He had a leg missing. I phoned the woman who had placed the ad. She told me that Sasha had belonged to a friend of hers who had emigrated to Australia. She had taken him in, but local youths had attacked and injured Sasha. That was why the leg had been amputated. 'We got another cat to keep him company but it hasn't worked out — now Sasha has disappeared.'

I wrote up the story and Jim sent a photographer to Sasha's home. I said I wanted a photograph of the other cat sniffily walking round the empty basket, for a caption that would read: 'I don't care if he never comes back.'

It didn't work out as neatly as that but it looked well. This wasn't my first story but it was the first story I was congratulated on — the first evidence to my colleagues that I had a journalistic instinct.

*Jinxed Cat Has Had Enough*

'Fucking good story!' muttered Sean, the managing editor, to Jim, almost out of my hearing. 'Fucking good story!'

The journalistic knack was to find a phrase which lifted a story above the ordinary. Jim asked me to interview Tommy Magee, a Protestant socialist who lived near me in Andersonstown. Tommy and his family had been visited by gunmen in their living room. They were moving out. Their story was the story of hundreds, perhaps thousands, of people in the city.

Jim said to me: 'Tommy is called the Lord Mayor of Andersonstown.'

'I never heard that before and I live there.'

'Well, some people call him that. Use it in the story.'

But what could I have brought to the story from my own experience? The knowledge that other Protestants lived in Andersonstown and had not been intimidated. It was strange to be affecting the role of the detached journalist in my own neighbourhood. Yet I came away from Tommy and his wife wondering if I had read events around me properly and if we Catholics were too blithely overlooking the threat to Protestants who lived among us.

On Saturdays, the paper functioned like a daily, and the reporters, who had been writing features or background pieces through the week, had to take on the hard news for the following morning. The army press office kept us informed of the latest bomb attacks and shootings around Northern Ireland, mostly in Derry and Belfast. Occasionally after a routine briefing, the press officer would add, in a solemn tone: 'and we have news now about Corporal so-and-so, shot on such and such a road last Thursday while on patrol. Corporal so-and-so passed away at 11 a.m. The GOC [General Officer Commanding] has sent his condolences to the family.'

I learnt, on these calls, how to affect the appropriate sympathy for a victim neither I nor the press officer actually knew. I had little enough sympathy to spare for dead and wounded soldiers when their dealings with me on the street were often provocative and rude. I doubted whether, if news of the shooting of a neighbour of mine had been broken in the officers' mess, there would have been much sympathy there either.

Jim and Paddy knew the press officers personally and their gossip about them centred mostly on one called Colin Wallace. Colin Wallace's strange behaviour persuaded them that he was probably a high-ranking intelligence officer but they weren't sure that he wasn't just a clown. They had met him in different uniforms, affecting different ranks. Wallace, years later, was imprisoned for the manslaughter of Jonathan Lewis, a Brighton antiques dealer, and claimed that he had himself been set up by the intelligence services. He was acquitted after serving six years in jail, and Paul Foot wrote a book, *Who Framed Colin Wallace?* This book credited Wallace's claims that the intelligence services had incriminated him in an attempt to silence his claims about their propaganda war in Northern Ireland.

One night, I took a call from Major Barry Brooking of the Royal Green Howards Regiment, stationed in north Belfast. It felt dangerous just to be talking to him. Certainly neighbours and friends would not have considered that I would, in the course of my work, be talking civilly to a plummy British army officer like the ones who raided their homes, searching for arms and people on the run.

Major Barry took a liking to me.

'You should come up and have a drink with the chaps in the mess.'

'Ah, I don't think so.'

'Love to have you — even drop you off home afterwards. Where do you live?'

Even telling him where I lived didn't dissuade him, yet if local republicans had spotted me being dropped off at night by British soldiers, they would certainly have shot us or tried to. And if they had failed, they would have shot me later. I knew that. Did Barry Brooking not know that? It seemed inconceivable to me that he might not.

Occasions for being friendly with soldiers and policemen were the most awkward for me, not because I shared the animosity towards them, expressed by many Catholics, but because of a mix of feelings. For a start, I was afraid of them. This man talking pleasantly to me now on the phone might well be frisking me brusquely on the street tomorrow. Worse still, he might be frisking my companion while being civil to me. I also knew that when we got beyond the civilities into conversation, we would be in danger of arguing. Yet I also feared that these people were more confident in their assumptions than I was in mine. I might be too easily converted. I might lose my allegiances and even my security in a lax moment of agreement.

Yet if I was being coy to spare others, few were being coy to spare me.

Columnists who wrote for *The Sunday News* would pass through the newsroom on their way to the editor's office and would sometimes stop to exchange comments with the reporters about the events of the day. One day, after news had come that an IRA sniper had shot dead a soldier, Patrick Riddell walked fretfully in. Patrick was a tight and emphatic little man who used to write in racial terms that would not be acceptable today — for instance, about the distinctive characteristics of the native Irish stock. He was furious about the shooting of the soldier. The anger was bursting out of him. He just couldn't contain it until he reached the editor's desk. He stopped in the middle of the newsroom and spun around, his fists clenched, his head jerked back, and scowled: 'The IRA are a disease-carrying vermin; they have never fought the British army and they never will.'

Who was he arguing with? With whom was he competing to express the deeper and more coherent revulsion? When people said things like this, I felt as if I were under attack, as if I were being challenged to agree with what they said. I did not agree with the IRA shooting soldiers but I couldn't agree that Kane, Gorman, Toland and the others were 'disease-carrying vermin'. If that is what they were, I was sure to have been infected myself already by proximity. I might even infect Patrick himself if he lingered in the room.

And you shoot vermin, don't you? You don't concede any reason or feeling to it; you simply expunge it.

But how were the Protestants even to know which Catholics threatened them and which didn't, which would go home and pass information on to a brother or friend who was a bomber, and which would never do such a thing, even under pressure? I would only have had to cross the street from my own front door to give the men of the most active company in the IRA any information they wanted about the people I worked with.

*The Sunday News* tried to position itself to appeal to

Catholic readers, and the selection of a mixed staff was deliberate. Still, unionists saw it as their paper since it belonged to Century, the group that owned *The News Letter*, and there were embarrassing moments for unionists who forgot how the culture of the office changed on a Saturday night. One Saturday, a unionist MP, Tom Caldwell, came into reception and asked to speak to a reporter. Jim sent me down to talk to him, probably guessing the likely result.

Tom wasn't a bad man. He was regarded as a liberal unionist and would later make his name as an art dealer. I had been in the same Business Studies class as his daughter two years before this. He didn't know that, but he was immediately friendly, a little drunk. He went on at length about a story he had. A Protestant man had been shot dead in east Belfast by loyalist paramilitaries. Tom had come from a meeting of local community representatives who had drawn up a statement for the press, essentially asking Protestants to keep their attention on the threat from the IRA and not to be fighting among themselves.

'It's so important — at this time — don't you think?'

I heard him out and took a statement, and, as we parted, he shook hands with me and asked my name. Here was a helpful reporter; it would be useful to have his name when he had to call again.

'Malachi O'Doherty.'

Tom paused. Ah, it sank in. He realised now that he had been talking to a Catholic as if he were a Protestant. He had let himself down. If he had been sober, he would have got my name first. He recovered himself quickly though. 'Well, a great pleasure meeting you, Malachi. Do your best now, won't you?'

He probably head-butted the door when he got outside.

What had shocked me about Tom Caldwell was that his statement seemed at odds with his presentation of himself as a liberal. With the sort of skills I was learning in *The Sunday News*, I could have coined a headline for his story that would have hurt him.

*Caldwell Asks Loyalists to Save their Bullets for the* IRA

His anxiety that loyalists were killing Protestants amounted to a preference that they kill others instead, and this was an inappropriately qualified statement about murder, from a public representative. To be fair, maybe if he had been sober, he would have thought it through himself.

Jim's strategy for teaching me to write in the house style of *The Sunday News* included throwing my work back at me and telling me it was shite. He was usually right. An early story he asked me to do was about how the IRA was using hired cars taken out with forged driving licences.

In my first draft, I wrote in the first person: 'I asked the manager of McCausland's....'

Paddy would have whispered, so as not to embarrass me, 'We don't use the first person for news stories.'

Jim roared: 'The fucking story isn't about you — it's about the fucking IRA. Who the fuck are you that anyone cares what you think?'

Paddy sat with me one day and explained the basics.

'No details in the first paragraph. The second paragraph always begins with "and" or "but". Don't worry about grammar. No big words.'

I was writing a story about the risks of a new flu vaccine. I wrote that a doctor had said there were no risks, except for a small number of people who were allergic to egg white. Jim, in a calmer moment, said: 'Write: "but even he admitted that for those who are allergic to eggs, the vaccine might blah blah —" okay?'

And that's how we did it, exaggerating everything but doing it through the choice of words with which we set up quotes when we couldn't do it through the quotes themselves. Thc doctor had no sense of having 'admitted' anything and phoned me after the story was published to tell me so.

# Chapter 4

*The Sunday News* had been established in the mid-1960s to get a share of an expanding Catholic market and, I think, to provide a slightly less salacious paper than the *News of the World* of which a more puritan Northern Ireland was wary. Still, the Christine Keeler scandal had introduced sex as legitimate content of the news story and *The Sunday News* saw itself providing more of it. Then came the violence of 1969 and after, and this strange hybrid paper evolved, with riot scenes and bomb damage on the front page and pictures of near-naked models on the inside.

I doubt if there was one mind that had conceived *The Sunday News*. It had been launched in the mid-1960s before the violence had started. At that time, it had been possible to imagine that a unified Northern Ireland identity was emerging. At least, a newspaper which did not affront Catholics or desert Protestants might sell to both. There was a market there, larger than either one community could provide. And people were interested in glamour, sport, entertainment and folksy stories about rural life. They were interested in what would come to be called lifestyle. They would read women's pages which told them how to organise a dinner party or prepare an outfit for a wedding on a budget. The men would want reviews of new cars. Soon this basically shy paper would find itself covering the major weekend atrocities.

Later, bombers would discover that Saturday evening was the worst possible time to attack because it was too late for the London and Dublin Sunday papers. But then, in the early 1970s, they would decide it was the ideal time. If the bombers were news-conscious at all, they were probably timing their attacks for us. Fortunately that thought never occurred to us. At least, it never occurred to me.

The important reader at home on a Sunday morning, sitting down with the paper after church or dinner, was presumed to be a man. The glamour shots we published for him seem mannered and modest now. I think they looked mannered and modest then too, though it would have been unthinkable to publish a picture of a bare breast or bottom. In the pictures supplied for us by the photo agencies, bikini bottoms were wide-banded at the sides and usually of a bunched or crumpled fabric rather than skin hugging. Bottoms were never wet. Clefts were never deep; wedgies were out. The last thing our bikini girls were dressed for was a swim. The make-up and stylised hairdos made that clear.

Our male reader would have been interested in guns and terrorism but would not have been familiar with the modern icons and vocabulary which suggested that violence, such as we were suffering, was a global infestation. Terrorism was just a make-do word for political violence then. It distinguished it from ordinary murder but only by a little, and morally it judged it worse, subhuman. Our male reader, the paper assumed, wanted to be shocked by the scale of the violence on the front page but, once he turned that page, he did not want to be greatly disturbed by it any more. He did not want to read evidence of a society which had been seriously damaged. Our little articles about the network for supporting men on the run, which explained the decoy cars, or the story about the life of an interned student, will neither have riled him nor informed him very much.

The reader's wife would have the woman's page. Women columnists, like Renee and Angela, would share with her their fears about the future, along with their design concerns. So the paper was almost a model of the society it reported, a society threatened by enormous, inexplicable and unexpected violence but which felt, at heart, safe and unruffled in its petty concerns. Our reader was free to plan a holiday, to move house, to contemplate a changed diet, to ogle girls' bottoms or marvel at those lovely little furry animals in the zoo, while the city was bombed to our deadlines and no one knew why — not even a Westminster MP for a local constituency, who thought we were being invaded by the Russians.

Jim would mediate to us the editor's idea of what the paper should be. He — Pat — was in a separate office with his secretary, Gwen, and had little to do with us. One day, Jim came down and said: 'You know, you lot are getting it too easy because of the troubles. What if all this stops? Where will we be then? Pat thinks we are losing the ability to go out and find stories — good smutty stories. I want to see more smut. Got it?'

I had no idea of how to find smut, but Jim had instincts.

There was that little story in one of the provincials about a young woman who had set up her own boutique at her home in County Down. I phoned her and arranged to bring Trevor, a photographer, with me. Trevor was a few years older than me and vastly more experienced as a journalist. He had a slightly gnarled manner but he was also interested in the job. Like all the other photographers, he was from a unionist background and, like most working journalists, he could be quick and clichéd in his judgment of people.

We went to a wealthy family home to meet a mother and

daughter. The mother was aloof but she brought us in and sat at a remove as the young woman proudly showed us samples of her design work. Trevor eyed the place as thoroughly as if he were planning to steal something. Then we went out to a converted garage where the young woman's clothes were on display. It was a cold, wet, rainy, late-autumn day. I wondered what chance there was that people would travel out here to buy a blouse or a belt, but the girl was ambitious. So was Trevor.

'If you've got all the details you want,' said Trevor, 'you can go back into the house while we get on with this.'

So I edged back round the door and sat with the prim mother, avoiding any coherent conversation about, say, the fact that we were now at war, and wondered what was keeping Trevor. I felt small there because, compared to our family, these people were rich and they were mannered in a way that seemed to go along with that.

Eventually Trevor and the girl returned and we said our goodbyes.

'Class bird that,' said Trevor. Oh, was he going to brag about how he had got on with her? 'I got some great shots there.'

He said that once I had left them in the garage, he had coaxed the girl into a little glamour modelling. 'She made me promise not to publish them, just to send her some copies.' He said he would show me some of them but he didn't, so I was confident that he was spoofing.

That Saturday, we were in the office, monitoring the crackly police radio, as we did every Saturday, when Jim let out a loud 'Fuck!'

He was reading the *Belfast Telegraph* and saw a picture of the boutique girl.

'That was our exclusive. Bitch!'

I was still the office junior but I thought I could judge that it wasn't really much of an exclusive anyway. Then Jim phoned Trevor. 'Have you still got the tit shots of that boutique girl? I want to see them. ... Well, promises count for nothing when she's gone to the *Tele* as well. Dig them out.'

So, that poor girl will have opened *The Sunday News* the following day, over the breakfast table, in front of her mother and the man she had recently married, to see herself in one of the sexiest pictures that had yet appeared in the paper. It showed her sitting in a suede dress which was tied loosely under her cleavage, and with her knees raised to open wide a split along the thigh.

'She should know the rules,' said Jim.

My extended caption quoted the girl: 'I like to make things that are a little outrageous,' she had said: like a handbag depicting a dog with one leg against a tree and a fat alley cat blowing bubbles with chewing gum.

*The Sunday News* in 1971 showed no sense of understanding that a feminist revolution was under way.

'Attractive Nulagh Harrold' — a former Miss Craigavon — was trying to join the all-male local branch of the Chamber of Commerce. Nulagh demonstrated her suitability for the Chamber of Commerce with her thighs, by sitting on a railing in white hot pants and high boots, in a tight blouse and with a big smile. A member of the Chamber of Commerce told the paper that he didn't think it was 'advanced enough for women members'. He needn't have worried; it didn't look as if Nulagh was very advanced either.

The modern feminist would be shocked by the story about '20-year-old English beauty queen' Susan Doughtrey, who was over in May 1972 to spend a weekend in Long Kesh as a guest of the 13/18 Hussars. Susan was a clerk at a steelworks in Rotherham and she posed for the photographer in what looked like a band uniform, pleated skirt and shirt with epaulettes, sitting on a sandbag wall while a dour-faced squaddie with his rifle appeared to examine her exposed knee with suspicion — suspicion perhaps that this was as close to Susan as he was going to get.

*The Sunday News* then was strangely detached from the troubles and even from normal life in Belfast. The reporters contributed very little content to it, proportionally. Even at times of extreme violence and unrest, the inside pages would carry syndicated features about Pakistan or the history of the Nobel Prize. We had a syndicated problem page, *Dear Abby*, which would never have been commissioned if the paper had really been trying to communicate to the native culture. It seemed that even here, the point was to offer a vision of a different world of more pedestrian concerns. It was the job of Leslie the sub-editor to take this American feature and translate it into the local idiom. He wasn't thorough. Perhaps he didn't feel the need to be. *Dear Abby* was like a running soap opera of American domestic life, not a sounding board for the real worries of our readers.

> Dear Abby, we are the parents of a 21-year-old son. After school he went to university and now he has a good job about 70 miles from here.
>
> He phoned us recently and said he was engaged and was bringing his girl to meet us on the weekend. We were so excited I could hardly wait because Larry hadn't been out with many girls.
>
> Well, when Larry and his girl walked in I nearly fainted. Abby, she is so fat! Should we say something to our son? Like suggest that he tell her to go on a diet? I just hate to think of that girl going down the aisle in a white gown and veil to marry our son!
>
> *Heartsick*
>
> Dear Heartsick: the way she 'looks' is only half the problem. The condition of her health is the other half. Tell your son (privately, of course) that you like the girl, but you hope she does something about her weight while she is still young. But bear in mind, he may have already spoken to her about it.

So, for Abby, looks and health were the whole problem. What about the problem of an interfering mother? What about the right of the woman to be fat if she wanted to be? Abby saw nothing questionable about the presumption of a man's right to tell his girlfriend to go on a diet.

*The Sunday News* was, essentially, an eccentric response to the violence of that time. It was a strange mix of self-improvement and coy lechery. The large syndicated profiles were of a kind that you might have found in a popular encyclopaedia. The violence was splashed over the front page, usually with a large picture of bomb wreckage. Yet inside was a quieter world of genteel people who focused on the good life and smaller problems.

Our readers were credited with a strange mishmash of concerns.

They read Abby to know if they should take a chance on romance with somebody who sounded nice on the phone but might look like a horror in person. One week, a feature on moving house dealt with the stress it might put on your marriage; the next we might be introduced to a family who was happy to have moved, and had been thinking of it even before their child was injured by a ricochet.

There was a social conscience element to our work too. Jim often made calls to government offices for people, to scare them into action — though aware that if the office responded, there would be no story at the end. And he encouraged me to do the same. The Housing Executive still hadn't done repairs for a family. We'd phone up, say we were doing a story about the family, and the repairmen would be out within hours. We exercised a right to harass the world. Sometimes we got into raging arguments on the phone. I called up a builder who was replacing the window catches on 300 houses in one estate. Every house had an ill-fitting catch. I had heard the story in a pub from the man hired for the job.

'Publish that and I'll sue you,' said the builder.

'Please do,' I said and laughed at him.

Across the table, Stephen the Canadian would be hectoring some other official. 'Excuse me; isn't this supposed to be a democratic country? Aren't you a servant of the people? Then you have no right not to answer my question, have you?'

And Jim would be slamming his phone down and shrieking: 'Fuckers! I am going to nail those fuckers.'

And then the bomb alarm would sound again and we would groan and shuffle out through the narrow corridors, past the compositors and through the print room and into the backyard to await the all-clear. And we would always come back to see that our office had not been searched at all, that everything was where it had been. Everyone knew that when the IRA did choose to bomb us, they would do it without telling us first.

# Part Two

# Chapter 5

There were nights then when I didn't sleep for the intense gunfire in the streets. One of the worst was the night Rita O'Hare was wounded during an attack on an army patrol and nearly got killed. Rita was a young red-haired mother whose husband I knew better than I knew her. Gerry drank in the same bars, argued politics and had a brash humour. I had been to parties in their house at which celebrities of the civil rights marches mingled; at which people jumped out the kitchen window or burnt bits of paper in the sink when an army patrol was spotted by lookouts. A lot of private parties in those days had lookouts.

Even just a couple of shots can unnerve you so that you can't sleep. A gunshot has such a definite sound. It seems to express its intention, abrupt damage — now. I would hear the low whine of army Saracens cornering into the street, the shouts of English accents: 'Put your fucking lights out!'

The IRA men were supposedly our defenders. Nearly everyone who has written about the IRA in that period agrees that it was a defensive organisation. This is nonsense. You don't feel defended — that is, made safer — when neighbours with guns are shooting at army patrols and retreating into your garden. Tommy Gorman's recollection of that time is that he and the others in E Company had to go out looking for targets — that the army wasn't coming to them. Once he took a pistol from a dump and walked out into the middle of the Andersonstown Road, a busy main road into town, and aimed at the back of an army jeep and pulled the trigger. The gun wasn't loaded. He ran away up St Agnes's Drive. No one noticed him.

One morning, Jim said to me, 'You look exhausted. Go home to bed.'

I walked down Finaghy Road North. It was a sunny day, mid-morning, not the time I was used to seeing life on the street. Suddenly I heard a loud double shot nearby. And another. Children ran around the corner and a woman in a doorway called them to her. I joined in, feeling foolish for being the oldest one, and she acknowledged my discomfort with a smile. One of the wee boys explained: 'That's an Armalite. He's firing at a helicopter.'

Had the gunman no fear of bringing a helicopter crashing down on streets where children played? Perhaps he didn't really believe he had a chance of hitting it. I doubt if he had.

It is terrifying when you don't see the gunman, and easier to manage your fears when you do. One day, I was walking down Slievegallion Drive on to the Andersonstown Road. This time, the shots passed right over my head. I glanced quickly to my left and saw an armoured personnel carrier, or pig as we called them, on the road, with rifles pointing through the rear-door slats and smoke from their barrels. I looked to my right and saw the bullets from those guns ricocheting off the wall of a white brick house, under the bedroom windowsill. I saw the barrel of an old rifle poke round the opened window frame, a bolt-action Lee Enfield 303, I think.

Okay, this was danger. Even if no one chose to shoot directly at me, one of those ricochets might hit my head and

I would go the way of baby Angela Gallagher. I turned behind me, looking for cover. Three or four small boys who had been playing there were calmly debating what they should do. Some wanted to lie down.

'Lie down along the wall,' I said. They would do it if I did it. We crouched low. I felt as self-conscious doing this as I always did, though it was hardly behaviour I would need to explain. Was it even a practical thing to be doing, though? Might I not look like a gunman taking cover? Anyway it was over in seconds. The shooting had stopped before I was flat on the ground. A woman was at the window now, checking the damage. Had she had any choice in the matter of her home being used like this? And suddenly people around me were in a panic. It was as if I had stepped into another world. Other people. They were enveloped in an entirely different atmosphere from the one I moved in. An old school friend, Philip, grabbed my arm: 'What's happening?'

For him, it was still happening.

I said, 'It's over.'

I had seen everything and my imagination hadn't leapt in to explain what I couldn't see, the way his had. It is wrong to suppose that courage or cowardice determine how someone will behave under fire. Information does.

At home, my mother told how she had stood at the kitchen window, watching Machine-gun Kate firing from behind a gable wall. 'The nerve of her! She just stood there shooting.'

'Maybe it was all for show and there was nobody there to shoot back.'

When the army came into our street at night, women rattled bin lids on the road or blew whistles to alert anyone who might be in danger of being arrested. The men of E Company would scatter. On a mischievous notion, one morning on the way to work, I bought a whistle from a sports shop near the City Hall, and carried it in my pocket all day, not showing it to anyone. I fiddled with it in private, balancing the pea on the vent and imagining it rattling inside. I presumed it wasn't a real pea. I had no plan to join the women on the street but I was keen to accept some opportunity to use the whistle. The more I handled it, the more I felt like giving it a good blast. There was no sense to this. I had no wish to warn the IRA and help the boys to escape, though I was frightened by the army raids. The soft whine of a Saracen armoured personnel carrier rounding into the street always signalled trouble, and I suppose I could rationalise now that blowing a whistle to deter them was better than leaving others to shoot at them. Blowing whistles might get rid of the soldiers, by making their work impossible, whereas shooting at them only drew them in.

But I wanted to blow a whistle some night only because it looked like fun, mildly dangerous fun. And having it didn't amount to a resolve to blow it; I could always just leave it in a drawer and forget about it, couldn't I? Maybe I intended only to dare someone else to do it. I don't know.

In any case, one night my father came into my bedroom and told me that there were soldiers in the garden. The silent night patrols were nicknamed duck squads. I was a bit drunk. I had had three pint bottles of brown ale with a retired schoolteacher in the next street. I opened the window and looked out. I saw nothing. Ha! Now was my moment. I retrieved my whistle from a drawer and blew a good shrill blast into the darkness. Silence. No harm done. There had been something of parody about it. See how ridiculous we look.

Then there was a sudden thud and another. I couldn't work out what it was. It was loud. My father and brothers, alarmed at my stupidity, gathered on the landing, working out that the thudding was the sound of a soldier kicking in the back door of the house. I thought: 'Oh, God, you've thrown everything away.'

I went to the head of the stairs as the door clattered open.

The soldier was huge. His face was blackened and he held his rifle by the stock. He was wrong for a living room. He reduced it to a public space. I was not afraid; I was numb. The first thing to do was step forward and own up, the way I would have done at school, since to let anyone else take a beating for this would be unforgivable. With one hand, the soldier clenched my shirt neck, twisted it to choke me and lifted me off the floor. My mother, in her nightie, was shrieking at him. I have a strange third-person perspective memory of this, which can't be right. But I have.

The soldier dragged me out into the back garden where his men were standing around waiting. 'I'm going to shoot you, Paddy.' He positioned me against the wall and pointed his rifle at me. Again I was past complaining but I said: 'Can't we do it over there, so that it doesn't go through the wall?' I moved away from the house.

He kicked me. 'Stupid bastard.' He dragged me by the hair around to the front of the house, through the hedge, and kicked me in the head when I fell. I was still too stupid to feel anything. My shirt was torn off my back. My nose was bleeding.

The soldiers stood me facing their pig and one of them unhooked an earthing chain below it which produced a sparkling pink and blue flame when it touched the ground. I would have let them do anything to me. They spread my legs and positioned me with my fingertips against the vehicle. One of the fingertips went in behind a shutter levered from the inside. A soldier amused himself by closing it tight over the finger. He then opened it again to see what I had made of that.

'Do you need to?' I said — or something like that. He decided he didn't wish to guillotine my finger after all.

Then I felt the electric current. This was supposed to be strong enough to throw off a mob scrambling over the vehicle or trying to overturn it. It wasn't. I have since experienced the shock from a cattle fence. I touched a wire with the tips of my fingers and felt an instant kick in the small of the back. I felt nothing from that armoured vehicle but a light tingle in my fingers.

They barked questions at me but there was no pattern or reason to them.

'What's your name?'

'Where is the IRA?'

'Who is in the IRA?'

I said: 'I am a journalist.'

Then I had an idea.

'Ask Colin Wallace.'

I had taken about eight of the little shocks by then.

'Oh, fuck off,' said the soldier who had dragged me there.

I stood up straight and looked at them.

'Go on.'

I wondered if they might shoot me in the back and say I had tried to escape so I walked to the house. They didn't shoot. I walked back across our neighbour's garden to the hedge, thinking it would be as easy to get through it again as it had been on the way out. It was much too high and dense to scramble over. This puzzled me. I had, after all, just been dragged through it.

Back in the house, no one was blaming me. They were just concerned for my cuts and bruises. A couple of local IRA men came in and asked what had happened. They might have been surprised that the soldiers had let me go but they didn't show it. At that time, many innocent suspects were being interned. I saw no reason why I should not have been taken too.

The next morning, I had a black eye. On the way to work, I bought a pair of dark glasses in a chemist's near the City Hall. Stephen laughed at me. 'How would you feel if you were a soldier in an IRA stronghold and someone blew a whistle on you? You could have got those guys killed. Aren't you ashamed of yourself, Malachi?'

# Chapter 6

Social life had changed in the housing estates. When rioting started in 1969, the pubs closed — sometimes because it was too dangerous for them to open, sometimes under a government order. Ministers imagined that they were facing a revolution on the streets because people were drunk on bright summer evenings.

Then when the IRA started its bombing campaign in 1970, it concentrated first on pubs. Some pubs had been burnt out during riots and those that survived, some gang or another blew up. A new type of commerce emerged — the drinking shebeen. Whether the IRA had planned to raise funds by knocking out the pubs and taking over the drinks trade, or whether it just happened that way, is one of many obvious questions I did not think to ask at the time. Like everyone else, I thought of the violence as something that was happening, not as something that was planned. Now there were shebeens everywhere, some with odd names like The Cracked Cup, some affiliated to one wing of the IRA, some to another, some associated with the group supporting prisoners or the Catholic Ex-Servicemen's Association.

There would be collections in these clubs for the Green

Cross, the fund for prisoners. It was a thoughtless choice of name for it; the Green Cross Code was the name given to a road-safety campaign on television, directed at small children. Occasionally I refused to give money to the Green Cross. It was my personal act of rebellion, as if I imagined I could be in that bar at all and not be supporting the cause. The entertainment in the clubs was always rebel songs: 'The Broad Black Brimmer', 'Four Green Fields', 'The Man from the Daily Mail'. Our neighbourhood was being taken through a rapid induction into republican culture with cheap drink and musical propaganda.

Once, in a bar in Belfast, we heard a bomb explode some streets away. Without knowing whether anyone had been killed or injured, most people cheered. It would have been easy to spot those who hadn't. The shebeens were a medium for purveying a party line, establishing the argument against criticism. The press would moralise about the death of a child killed by a ricochet. The counter arguments were blunt: Sure, what do you expect in a war? We didn't start this. Accidents happen. You're one to talk.

A popular voice emerged and it was a counter-moralising voice.

'Well, how do you think the guy that did it feels?'

It was important — for the revolution to continue — that those of us who did not participate should doubt that we had a right to criticise. In this climate of cynicism, a journalist might be persuaded that he was defending the superficial perspective and missing the common sense of the street and the bar. But that common sense was as artificially conditioned in the service of a political interest as any government or army propaganda.

What this was really about was taking sides: if you were on the side of the state or the unionists, you bemoaned the slaughter by the IRA and absolved the killings by the army. If you were on the side of the IRA, you bemoaned only killings by others. And if you lived alongside the IRA and did not want to side with them, you held back your instinctive moral rejection of bombings and murders and the blithe use of weapons that led to the deaths of children, for you knew what the answer would be: 'Aye, you would have us in subjection. It's all right for you; you've got a job. Who the fuck are you to talk that never did anything?'

Sooner or later, if I stayed in Belfast, I *would* be required to do something, to hide a gun, run a message. At night, my dreams recycled this anxiety: soldiers frisked my body or searched my room and I was appalled to discover that I had a gun that I could not hide. A Freudian would say this gun was my erection or a secret homosexual yearning. In Belfast then, a young man could take his dreams literally.

My social life was confined then to bars in which I felt safe. That's not to say they were safe bars. I developed a habit of going straight from the office to Kelly's Cellars in Bank Street. This was a dingy old pub in which the eighteenth-century revolutionary Henry Joy McCracken was said to have hidden. It had an atmosphere of banditry. The seats along the bar were old barrels. The wooden bar itself was so battered and scratched, it would have made no appreciable difference how roughly you treated it. If you were in early, you could get an empty cubicle and hold it for your friends coming later.

Kelly's attracted journalists like myself, Jim, Kevin, Liam; it attracted an arts crowd; it attracted thieves like Billy, who could sell you a jumper or even take orders for different sizes; it attracted militants, some Provisional IRA, some Official IRA. It did not inspire sufficient loyalty in them to discourage them from occasionally planting small bombs there, though they were civil enough to phone and say that they had done it, so that the place could be cleared.

Kelly's became like a second home to me. In fact, I was probably spending more time there than I was at home. I would go in after work for a pint with the afternoon crowd and sometimes find myself sitting through the evening when it was almost empty before the night crowd came in. The barman cashed my cheques and I had a big shock when the bank returned these to me in batches of dozens. They were the plainest statement possible about my life. I earned a professional salary — not a mere living wage — and spent most of it in one pub.

Another pub I went to in the evenings was the Old House in Albert Street. The Old House had music — folk bands for urban republicans who imagined they were qualified by their roots to indulge the sea shanty.

*Wrap me up in me oilskins and jumper.*

I drank every day then, a minimum of a couple of pints at night, frequently a couple at lunchtime or after work, often going on with Maguire after the pubs closed, to someone's house — someone we met in the pub — maybe a neighbour. Which meant that I often couldn't recall in the morning how I had got to bed the night before. Or a scrap of memory might survive the fug, like one I have of rattling down a hill on an old bicycle. Presumably I was alerted by the speed and danger and rose to conscious consideration of what I was doing, and that is how an imprint was made. Otherwise I was taking nothing in. Memories are lost sometimes, not because they are erased by drink and time but because they were not registered.

Maguire might fill me in the next day. 'You nearly started a fight. You were paying too much attention to your man's daughter; he didn't like it.'

One morning, I woke up naked under a blanket in a house in Cavendish Street, having been to the Old House the night before. Had someone undressed me? I had no idea. I let myself out and got the bus home. My mother was working day shifts at the hospital then and had already left. The news said that a man had been shot and dumped in the St James area. My father made me a cup of tea. 'Phone your mum and tell her you're okay. She went out thinking that was probably you.'

It could as likely have been me as anyone else. Indeed, a man who threw himself drunk on the mercies of Belfast most nights was at greater risk than those who sat at home and watched the news. One night, walking up the Falls Road with my two brothers, after the Old House had closed, I heard a soft English voice say, 'Halt or I fire.'

It sounded like a joke. It was voiced like a bland statement. I heard it a second time in the same flat tone. I turned around and saw a soldier down on one knee, pointing his rifle at me. He had spoken not to be heard, but minimally to fulfil a legal requirement. I walked back towards him.

'You were hoping we wouldn't stop, weren't you?'

He laughed nervously. I got the impression that this was his first time playing this game. An officer took our names and let us go.

Belfast was dangerous. On another evening, I went with my friends Maguire and Fegan in Maguire's car up to Ardoyne to meet some girls I knew from Kelly's. A joint police and army patrol waved us down. A police officer questioned us while the soldiers stood by. We were from Andersonstown. Where were we going?

'Looking for a party.'

Where?

We didn't say. When you were nabbed by the police, you only made it bad for others if you gave their names and addresses. They decided to take us in. The police ordered me into the back of their vehicle. A soldier took my place in the front of Maguire's car and followed us to Tennent Street police station on the Shankill Road. This wasn't right. To take us from a republican area into a loyalist area was endangering us.

I sat on a side bench in the back of the jeep. I kept quiet and avoided their eyes, but as we moved off, I felt a poke in my ribs. I looked at the policeman beside me. He was jabbing me with his finger. I would have smelt of drink and perhaps he hoped I was drunk and rash enough to react with sufficient annoyance to allow them to beat me up. That's how I read the problem. While I was looking straight in his face, he jabbed me sharply in the ribs again but under the cover of his coat so that the others facing us wouldn't see. So they weren't in on it.

'Please stop poking me. I don't see the point in it myself.'

The cop looked around to see how the others were reacting to this. They looked blankly at him, unimpressed, so he stopped.

At Tennent Street, as we stepped down from the jeep, Maguire's car was arriving behind us. The soldier in the front seat held his rifle across his lap. When we were alone in a room together, Maguire said, 'That soldier was crapping himself in case another patrol took him for an IRA man and opened fire on us.'

So the soldier had had no doubts that other soldiers would shoot first and enquire afterwards.

Such an inconvenience and risk to take three men to the Shankill Road! For what? We waited our turn to be questioned by an English officer about nothing in particular, and then we were released, one by one. Fegan and I waited for Maguire to come with the car and that was it, another night ruined. But later, Catholics released onto the Shankill Road to walk home were caught by loyalists and shot dead. The police and army, our protectors, had taken no particular care to spare us that.

Many young men were learning to drive by hijacking and stealing cars and either raking about for their own amusement or doing jobs for the IRA. Even a legitimate driver or learner had to acquire the same reckless habits to survive.

John Carlin, who had taught me business studies at

college, had a driving school now. One Saturday morning, before a lesson, I awoke to an enormous thump. The IRA had stolen John's car, packed it with explosives and detonated it under the M1 bridge at Finaghy. They hardly scratched the concrete but they broke my routine. And though the boys who had done that passed me on the street, I said nothing about it to them and they said nothing about it to me. In some sort of way, it was no business of either of us. Just the sort of thing that happens in war.

On a Saturday night, I answered the office phone to the manager of the Wellington Park Hotel. There had been an attack near the hotel but he wanted us to run a story that would say that it was still open for business. I took down his statement and then he said: 'Please come and have dinner here yourself some night, as my guest.'

So, on Wednesday, I put on my new bomb-damage sale shirt, and my father drove me down Castle Street to pick up Kate, a girl I had known from college and had recently bumped into again. At the hotel, we were treated like people who dined every night in nice hotels and expected the best tables. I had trout for the first time in my life. Should I eat the skin? I wasn't sure. My mother had briefed me on the correct use of the cutlery, from the outside in. Still I ate the soup with the dessert spoon because it was the same shape as the spoons I ate soup with at home.

'Never mind, sir. I'll fetch you another,' said the waiter.

I didn't get any more than pally with Kate. My problem was that I did not have a lair to bring a girl back to. It wasn't just the danger of moving through Belfast that restricted me. And I was unshapen still, not an adult, too self-conscious. I was stressed and confused and I needed to be kissed. I needed to be smothered and rubbed by a woman as urgent as myself, and any girl who looked at me could see that and backed off.

I was living every possible transition at once, from the Catholic world to the Protestant, from childhood to manhood, from amateur to professional, from working class to middle class, from being immortal to being mortal and vulnerable.

And I grew more at home in the strange world that journalism is.

My social life rarely intersected with that of my colleagues unless we had planned it that way. One day, I ran into Paddy and was impressed by his world. Maguire and I had been driving up the Lisburn Road from a pub when soldiers waved us down. Usually this meant bother of some degree. The soldiers had two civilians with them already, a man and a woman. The man, probably in his early twenties, seemed to be very drunk; he was unsteady on his feet. He was dressed in brightly coloured clothes, like a pop singer. His girlfriend had wispy long dark hair. They were hippies of sorts, I supposed.

The girl was distressed. She was obviously worried about the man, and the soldiers asked us if we could take them home. I'm guessing now that the man was drugged in some way and that if the soldiers had had to resort to calling the police for help, he and the girl would have been arrested. The soldiers could see that problem and wanted to help. That, in itself, was a surprise. I tried to steady the man with an arm across his back and, as I did, he unzipped his red cotton trousers. God, what would happen now? What happened was that Paddy turned up, dressed as if he had been to a party himself, in a flash crushed-velvet jacket of a style I determined then I would one day own myself.

'Problems, Malachi?' He was grinning.

The man had his penis out now, a large pale one, and he was holding it with no greater care than was enough to avoid splashing his own clothes. I steered him away from the others, bent him back a little from the waist and he slashed a high sparkling arc. Good pressure. Again I was wondering if I had slipped into a parallel universe in which soldiers wouldn't spontaneously kick a man who did that. When the man finished urinating, he slumped helplessly, and the woman bent and tidied his penis away. I was suddenly pining to know a woman who would make such easy acquaintance with my own.

The girl was able to tell us where they lived, and Paddy was able to explain to Maguire how to get there. The soldiers waved us all goodbye with the best of good wishes for a safe journey, and we took the drunk man and his girl in the car to a large ground-floor flat where other hippies were fretfully waiting for them. We helped them in, and the group of hairy men and women thanked us profusely. Had he been missing for hours? Had he been wandering around drugged? I would probably read a situation like that better now than I could then. The drunk man sat on the floor and another woman enfolded him in her arms, rocked him and wept. It was 1971. Anything could have happened to him out there. They weren't so trippy that they didn't know that.

But I went away thinking that there was another life to be had in Belfast besides the one we had been living ourselves. I wouldn't have minded moving in with those people.

# Chapter 7

It was autumn and then it was winter. I had been learning my way around Northern Ireland on stories culled from the provincial papers. The photographers took me protectively under their wing. We went to Armagh, Newry, Derry, Enniskillen and into remote countryside, looking for sculptors, hunters, plane-builders, collectors, musicians — anybody with a story, and almost any human activity could be a story. Once outside Belfast, we were beyond the troubles. Rural Northern Ireland was still mostly peaceful. Only in Derry might we see another barricade or more scorched tarmac. Yet in the early dark evenings, returning to the city was like descending into a pit. We would often come back to gridlock, the town frozen by one or two real bombs and a dozen hoaxes that cleared buildings and closed roads.

'The people who are making a fortune out of this,' said Farnum, the oldest of the photographers, 'are the glaziers. Makes you wonder if they are behind it.'

This was the sort of thing people said when they had no choice but to remark on the violence, yet no wish to say what they really thought. For unionists in particular, profit seemed a more feasible explanation of the violence than that bad government and discrimination had provoked it, or that idealistic young men were prepared to kill and die for an impossible political dream and out of loyalty to each other and their leaders. Of course, fortunes *would* be made out of the IRA campaign, not just through violent crime, but through insurance fraud, legal fees and police overtime, but the survivors of E Company that I have met since do not seem to have much to show for all their robberies. Many in the IRA would surely be rich if they had devoted their violence and wit to making money for themselves.

'Do you think that there will be a Protestant backlash?' I asked Farnum.

'It's already happening, isn't it?'

I wasn't sure. When Catholics anticipated a Protestant backlash, they imagined hordes of men descending on Catholic areas and killing hundreds of people in one night. There were loyalist gangs like the UVF, the Ulster Volunteer Force, which claimed continuity with the Ulster Volunteers formed in 1912 to resist Home Rule, and which had been wiped out at the Somme having enlisted in the 36th Ulster Division. There was the Ulster Defence Association which was evolving out of the vigilante groups that had been formed at the start of the troubles, ostensibly to defend Protestant areas. The common Catholic understanding was that these groups merged into the institutions of the state and that the British army's Ulster Defence Regiment, and the armed police force, the RUC, would one day combine with them to drive the Catholic population south. It never happened. Indeed, it is a wonder that people who dreamed that ghastly dream, who really believed it might come true, worked so hard to provoke it.

The backlash had started but it was the killing of random Catholics, one by one, or in groups, or in bombed bars. Even as this was beginning, we didn't notice. One night, Paddy and I drove into East Belfast because we had heard reports of gunfire around Short Strand. Short Strand was a small Catholic area on the east side of the Lagan. It was mythically talked about as a brave but vulnerable enclave. Was it under attack?

We got stuck at a loyalist vigilante roadblock. Months later, when the murder of Catholics became routine, I would have been unable to do this; I would have been sure I was going to die. Even in late 1971, this seemed not to be such an appreciable danger that no Catholic in his right mind would go where we were going. We waited in the queue of cars. The ones behind us made it impossible to turn around. Maybe we would attract suspicion if we tried. The gunfire just streets away was almost constant. It sounded like a major battle. The vigilantes at the barricade asked us for identification. They had no right to ask us for anything. All I had was a letter from the newspaper since my press card hadn't come through yet. 'To whom it may concern: Malachi O'Doherty is a bona fide representative....' It might as well have said: 'To anyone who cares: Malachi O'Doherty is a taig and a bona fide target.' Indeed, it didn't need to say anything other than my name to make that clear. The vigilante who questioned me was curly-haired and in his early twenties.

'Get out of here. It isn't safe.' Insisting on acting like a reporter, I asked him what he knew. He said that the IRA was attacking Protestant streets. He gave Paddy directions to streets that would lead us away from the line of fire.

Back at the office, I stood by a window in the dark stairwell and listened. The shooting continued. There must have been thousands of shots fired that night. I expected to hear the next day that dozens had died, and yet often in such battles nobody died.

Later in the year, I blithely walked through another interface, with my friend Maguire, just to see a little bomb damage — actually just to kill a couple of hours on a Sunday afternoon. Suddenly we were surrounded by young men.

Who were we? We started making up a story. We were from Suffolk, a Protestant area. A young housewife ran across the street, wiping her hands on a tea towel.

'Get them off the street,' she said.

If they did that, we would die, probably in pain, probably slowly. That's what was now happening to others.

An army pig came around the corner.

'Scarper,' said one of the lads.

'Youse are lucky today,' said the woman.

Certain deaths survive in detail in my memory from those days, as against hundreds that failed to register deeply.

In October, British soldiers shot dead two women driving through streets off the lower Falls Road, trying to alert the IRA that they were in the area. The women were from Cumann na mBan, which was known as the women's IRA, though Cumann na mBan was reputed to be proud of its integrity as a separate organisation from the IRA. There were other women in the IRA who were not members of Cumann na mBan. The army had come into the area to search houses and the women, with two other people, drove around a circuit of streets at four o'clock in the morning, blasting a foghorn. Other women beat bin lids on the pavement.

Soldiers had shot at the car.

This was a controversial killing because the victims were women and because it raised the question of whether or not it was legitimate for the army to shoot people who fled from them. Certainly the army had often opened fire on people who had ignored an order to stop. The British army claimed that before the soldiers opened fire, as the car screeched around a corner away from them, someone had broken the rear window and fired pistol shots at them.

The next day, the man who had been driving the car, William Davidson, held a press conference. He showed some of his own clothing with bullet holes in it. Someone had actually tape-recorded the shooting. *Sunday News* reporters heard that tape. They heard the bin lids. They heard the screech of the car evading the soldiers. They heard the rattle of automatic gunfire. They heard the pause and two further shots. No pistol.

The army said that no one who opened fire on them could expect not to be fired back at, not even women, though they promised to release pictures to show that the women were dressed as men. Major Christopher Dunphie told a press conference that the shooting was the result of 'despicable' action by terrorists using women on their missions. He said: 'One of my men saw a man crawl from the car with what he thought to be a pistol, but before he could open fire at him a crowd appeared.'

In the coming years, there would be many cases like this, where the army or police justified shooting people by claiming that they had first fired on them and it later became clear that they hadn't. Major Dunphie said that his soldiers were not the only ones to have mistaken the women for men. He said that the ambulance men had first pointed out that one of the dead was a woman, even when they still thought that the other was a man.

The army press office issued pictures of the dead women. These showed the women's faces blown out by bullets which had hit their heads from behind. The faces were like raw meat. We could publish them only with the wounds blacked over. A reporter gets to see things from which the public is protected. I felt sick looking at these pictures when Jim passed them round. I looked again and again to see if I could get used to the sight without a nauseous response. I was discovering a new feeling; I had never been disturbed in quite this way before. But what the army wanted us to see in the pictures was that the women were wearing fleecy check shirts and trousers with large belts, the sort of clothing working men would wear.

My sister Bríd with Eddie Dunning, the policeman she would marry. Both are now dead.

Barney, my father. He lived to a ripe old age and kept his beady eyed scowl to the end.

Stephen, Rick and me, standing (*left to right*). Eddie, the industrious one, still at his typewriter.

The speed ramp is where the Riverdale barricade stood. That is where Patsy McVeigh was shot. Frank McGuinness died near where the boys are, in the right of the picture.

There is nothing to suggest now that this street was the base from which many IRA ambushes and bomb attacks were launched.

## IRA men in dinghy spark off hunt

The finding of three members of the IRA in a dinghy in Cork harbour late last night sparked off intensive investigations in the area by the Army and Gardai.

Gardai swooped on the men, who were suffering from exposure, after they had been tipped off about suspicious circumstances in the Myrtleville area of the har-

## Living room jungle

If Tarzan had never found Jane he might quite happily have settled for Maire Stronge.

For Maire, a pretty young housewife, spends most of her day caring for a leopard and a Syrian brown bear.

But it isn't such a dangerous life. The bear, Oliver to his friends, and Shirley the leopard are still cubs and relatively harmless.

They belong to the Belfast Zoo at Bellevue but Maire and her husband John were asked by the Belfast City Veterinarian Dr. Joseph Gracey to look after them.

When Oliver was born his mother did not care for him so John and Maire volunteered as babysitters until the cub is big enough to look after himself.

While Shirley stalked along the back of the sofa, snarling like a mature predator, and Oliver hobbled, screamed and stamped his foot like a child with tantrums Maire was trying to say that they were both "really quite tame."

And in our picture Shirley the leopard seems to feel a bit left out of things while Maire finds that, even at a few months old, Oliver can give a strong affectionate bear hug.

Apologies to Máire, but I wrote that back in pre-feminist days.

# We will have no fresh food by the year 2,000

**Fresh meat, fruit and vegetables could be a thing of the past by the year 2000. And even if a supply of fresh food is available then it could become a luxury to those who could afford to pay extravagant prices.**

Increased prices already have a stranglehold on Britain's food market, which claims an annual turnover of more than £15,000 million.

Government statistics released last week state that the consumption of instant foods (frozen, canned and dried) is increasing at a rate of 7.5 per cent. per year.

By 1975, it is estimated, more than one third of the food market will be comprised of convenience foods.

Not only will hotels, pubs and clubs be serving up dishes from the deep freeze and cans but housewives will be forced to swallow their pride and serve exactly the same menus.

According to sales graphs in large food companies such as Birds Eye, Nestles and Cadbury the use of canned soups and vegetables has more than trebled in the past five years.

Recent surveys have shown that the price of fresh food has risen more rapidly than instand foods and researchers pessimistically predict that the only safety measure to control the rising prices in Britain is the Common Market.

"There is a ready supply of fresh foods on the Continent because the convenience boom has not caught on there yet and we hope this eventually will help the British market," one researcher said.

However, other sources claim the boom is catching on in European markets and experts from those countries are at present investigating the system in Britain.

## Advantages

At present the use of dried foods in Britain is rising at a rate of 10.5 per cent. and frozen foods at 10 per cent. And the growth rate or prepared food is 5 per cent. and canned food 4.5 per cent.

Caterers and hoteliers are relying more on convenience foods because they are more readily available, they keep, and apart from helping to cut down staff expenses, they can be served more cheaply to the customer.

It has also been stated that housewives have been so expertly brainwashed by te vision advertisements t they are buying convenier foods without even consid ing the thought of prepari fresh food.

One shopkeeper explain "Apart from the fact t few of them really kn how to cook, they just do have time to go through process of preparing a pot soup, fresh vegetables a meat and a little gravy. you watch some of them ing their shopping you wo think they didn't even ha time to select the right of soup."

Hoteliers and restaura managers claim that to p pare a complete menu of fr food is virtually impossible

"Fresh food is very exp sive and the customer wo be unable to pay the bill af the hotel expenses, etc., ha been taken into conside tion," said Mrs. H. Ton manageress of the Winds Hotel at Knocknagoney.

## Variety

She said it was the Hote policy to serve fresh fo whenever possible, especial for lunch, but at times would be virtually impossib to prepare a variety of fres food, particularly vegetables

"This happens mostly a functions when there is quit a variety of vegetables on th menu," she said

Some hoteliers admitted that 80 per cent. of the food served to guests was convenience food and in one instance a manager of a well reputed hotel refused to comment on the type of food prepared in his kitchen.

Of the guests spoken to in hotel dining rooms one commented: "I think Sunday dinner is the only meal I can say my wife serves up without having any tinned stuff in it, but I suppose she is too busy during the week to go through the long ceremony of washing and preparing everything."

# Operation clean-up for Lough

The National Trust is to organise a sponsored clean-up around the shore of Strangford Lough.

It hopes to involve more than 500 volunteers from schools, youth, scout and girl guide organisations and yacht clubs.

The venture is intended to give maximum publicity to the litter problem at the beginning of the holiday season.

Each group of volunteers will be invited to adopt, or will be allocated, a stretch of shoreline. They will be expected to clean this area of all litter on the appointed day, Saturday, May 6.

The volunteers will also seek sponsors for their task, getting written guarantees from as many people as possible who would be willing to contribute a sum of money per half-hour during which they are engaged in litter clearance. Supervisors would check the work and the money could then be claimed.

The National Trust aims to clean up all the shoreline on the same day. Forty per cent. of the money collected, after expenses have been deducted, may be allocated to a project of the groups own choosing, if it so wishes. The remainder will be used to promote conservation in the area through the Strangford Lough Wildlife Scheme.

The paper's policy was to find other things than the Troubles to be alarmed about.

We gave Martyn Turner his big break too.
(© Martyn Turner)

The wreckage of McGurk's bar. (© Victor Patterson)

A dead baby in a fireman's arms. This bombing on the Shankill was the IRA's retaliation for the bombing of McGurk's. (© Victor Patterson)

Robert Lindsay Mason, the eccentric unionist who took a council seat for the nationalist Falls Road, when nationalists were boycotting the polls in protest against internment.

A bad augur. Civil Rights marchers hammered by the army on Magilligan Strand, a week before Bloody Sunday.
(© Victor Patterson)

'As if they saw the buckle on the belt before they decided to shoot,' said Jim.

I took a phone call from a man who said he had seen the shooting.

'The first shot was at the rear tyre, just to stop the car. Then the other soldiers joined in, thinking the women were the target. It was all a big misunderstanding.'

'Can you give me your name? What were you doing there?'

He hung up.

He may have been a fantasist or a propagandist of some kind, trying to turn the story to suit his allies. Or he may have been one of the soldiers. The dead women were sisters, Maura Meehan and Dorothy Maguire. Maura had four children. Her husband got £1,200 compensation from the army over a decade later. Dorothy was 19.

# Chapter 8

The more experienced reporters on *The Sunday News*, like Jim and Stephen, also freelanced stories to other papers: Jim for the *Cork Examiner*, Stephen for an American news service. I aspired to doing something similar. Sometimes they would use details I gave them and they would pay me a cut of the fee. So any day you stuck your head around the office door, you might have seen Jim dictating his story to the copy-takers in Cork, with his familiar dramatic inflections, Stephen typing up his story for Canada, and me — well, me trying to make an appointment with the Cats Protection League or just phoning up my contacts for a chat to see if there was anything I could make a story out of.

'Anything at the zoo?' Jim asked.

'Naw. Though the leopard has just had a cub.'

'Wha!'

It was as if an alarm had been triggered. Sean, the managing editor, who could type with a cigarette between his fingers, froze.

'And you don't think that's a story?'

Well, Jim's story was about three IRA men having been found freezing in a dinghy off the south coast of Ireland. 'It looks to me like an effort to land weapons from a ship,' he said. 'The Provos are bringing in tons of gear from the States.'

My story was nothing like that.

'Get me the fucking leopard,' barked Jim. 'And get it before any of the other papers get it.'

The leopard story was even better than Jim had imagined. A zoo keeper's wife was bottle-feeding the leopard cub and a young Syrian brown bear called Oliver, in her home. She was relaxed in their company, but they terrified me. I sat on her sofa as the cat stalked my collar. I had been pawed by other cats before — after all, I had covered the Cats Protection League. This cat was strong. And suddenly Oliver was gripping me at knee height.

'He only wants to play.'

The woman with the leopard and the bear expected me to trust that I was safe in her living room with two wild animals and she thought my caution was just an irrational uppitiness on the part of a self-important hack. She'd read me correctly there, but I was still scared of the leopard and the bear.

The picture we published showed her with the two animals in her arms: Oliver licking her face, the leopard apparently trying to bite her shoulder.

I wrote, 'If Tarzan had never found Jane, he might quite happily have settled for Máire Stronge. Máire, a pretty young housewife, spends most of her day caring for a leopard and a Syrian brown bear.'

Had I not turned out something trite and sexist, someone else would have rewritten it.

*The Sunday News* did not publish an editorial. It wanted to appeal to both Catholic and Protestant communities and not to be identified with any political line. All opinion in the paper was from by-lined columnists. They included socialists, raving chauvinists, unionists and refined ladies who dealt with home and fashion. *The Sunday News* created the impression that it imagined a coherent and unified Ulster readership which was as intrigued by the left-wing liberalism of our urbane humanist, John D. Stewart, as by the right-wing vitriol of the raw angry racist Patrick Riddell. There was an audience for the opposites, so long as the contending positions were so extreme as to be amusing.

Riddell was a buffoon and was valued as a buffoon, not just to reassure Protestants that their position was well-represented, I suspect, but also to show Catholics that Protestant politics were histrionic and ludicrous. There was no serious political analysis in the paper, nor much sense of the continuity of the troubles; it just seemed to be one grisly thing after another, to emerge out of the same sort of human fickleness which produced road-traffic accidents and vandalism.

A girl being carried from a bombed building was photographed with her legs best displayed, for readers who were imagined to be only faintly interested in why she couldn't actually walk on those legs, yet very interested in how shapely they were. Two firemen carrying her appeared unsure where to look with all this uncovered female flesh in their arms. The photographer had no such problem.

Various lunatic theories tried to explain why Northern Ireland was now consumed by sectarian warfare. Were the Soviets at work destabilising us? One report said that Robin Chichester Clark MP planned to raise that very question in Westminster. No one perceived any plot or pattern behind the IRA. It was assumed to be simply impassioned and unreasoning, indulging in gestural politics alone. Monica Patterson of Women Together said: 'Our only message is peace — if any point was to be made by violence, surely it is made.'

Some news stories of the time suggest trends that the columnists and reporters missed. In the autumn of 1971, Ian Paisley was quoted on the front page predicting that

Westminster was about to dissolve the home parliament at Stormont and govern the region directly. He was right but he was out by four months. Still, he had understood that there was an attainable goal available for the IRA to work to. If instability was tempting the London government to dissolve the local one, and the IRA knew that and wanted that, it made sense for the organisation to maintain and increase its violence.

Another story reported a loyalist complaining that money being raised by vigilantes was being diverted into a central fund. What for? he wanted to know. This was surely a strong early hint that loyalists were organising a huge movement and preparing to buy weapons.

We had a story about timer switches being stolen from lampposts for bombs. Given that the street lights were out now all over Belfast, that augured a lot more bombing to come.

This detached tone of the paper gave no clue to the concerns and interactions of the journalists who produced it, to our quarrels and our black humour. All of us probably knew more about the character of the city than we were conveying in our writing, as we knew more about women and sex than we implied in the superficial, strangely moralistic captions we wrote for glamour pics. And we were a little universe of our own within that building, where nearly everyone else was Protestant and unionist. Our weekday office was remote from reception and the other newsroom, *The News Letter*'s. We were found down narrow corridors, up small winding staircases that took you deeper into the smell of old dust and machinery. Some of the men in the print room were loyalists. Our doorman became a leading public figure on a loyalist committee, yet he showed no animosity towards me. He tried to sell me watches.

My colleagues were a challenge to my assumptions.

A young brown-haired woman at reception, of an age and

build I would have fancied, and a demeanour — modest — that I would have felt confident approaching, was injured by a bomb, scarred in one leg. When she came back to work, I wondered whether I should comment on this or ignore it. Should I acknowledge that I feared she might think me close to the people who had bombed her, that she might be right in thinking that? Or should I say nothing, allow her no reasonable suspicion of me and try to remain confident that she understood that this had nothing to do with me? And to argue with myself that it had nothing to do with me, that I had no responsibility to reassure her, also felt wrong. So one day I said to her: 'I am sorry to hear about your injury. It's dreadful.'

I wondered afterwards if I had guiltily overstated my sympathy or failed to say what simple reason demanded: that nothing justified the scarring of vulnerable flesh. It seemed that no honest and worthwhile statement of sympathy with her was available to me; it would always come out wrong. And when I made my statement, she seemed embarrassed, as if she didn't know how to receive it either. It would have been much easier for a Protestant colleague to say simply, 'Fuck the bastard who did that to you' and to be credible in his anger. Had she been injured in a car crash, I could have said simply, 'You poor thing.' There was no etiquette established by which a Catholic might sympathise with a Protestant his neighbour had bombed.

One day, we were talking in the office about the IRA and I was expressing my disgust for them and for their bombs but trying to explain also why much of the criticism of them from others felt to me as if it implicated me.

'I am proud to be Irish,' I said.

'Why?' asked Stephen. 'What did you do to determine that you would be Irish?'

'Aren't you proud to be Canadian?'

'Not at all. I love Canada but that's another matter. I didn't choose to be Canadian, so I have no grounds for pride.'

'Ah yes, but you know what I mean.'

'No, I don't know what you mean. I think that's the problem with this fucking place — that people put all this weight on statements that don't mean a thing. I'd understand you if you said, "I like this place and I want to go on living here and I want it to be well governed." But that's a different thing.'

'Are you proud to be Irish, Jim?' I asked, looking for support.

'Don't rope me in. It was you started this. If you can't explain what you meant, then admit that you're beat and don't say it again.'

And I seriously did think about it, just to try to find a riposte for Stephen. I could not find one and decided to think before I spoke if I didn't want to be chewed up by these guys.

In different ways, my friction with them — with Jim, the cynical journalist; with Eddie, the quiet conscientious worker; with Rick, the reserved one; with Stephen, the freebooting traveller passing through; and with Paddy, the liberal intellectual — tempered all my thinking about who I was and how I related to the changes happening around me. This was an education. I had hardly noticed, of course, that Stephen was a Catholic too and felt vulnerable covering loyalist parades. Had I simply come in as the only Catholic in an office of Protestants who were as blunt as were many of those beyond the office door, in other parts of the building, I would probably have simply defended my Irish nationalism and even the IRA, where it seemed that those criticising them were doing it instinctively and without thought. But this was a richer challenge.

Still, I was argumentative, and I was easily drawn into quarrels I would lose.

'I reject that,' I would say and they would laugh.

'Why are you laughing, Rick?'

'Because you have taken the bait again.'

'What are you working on?' said Jim after lunch one day.

'Just a couple of fillers.' Fillers were stories lifted from provincial papers. I had moaned about doing them. Jim cut these out with a razor blade, glued them on to a sheet of pink copy paper and shared them out. We would rewrite them as stories a couple of inches long.

'When you've finished off, would you go and wash Pat's car?'

'Uh?' I was outraged and frightened. 'No, I won't.'

'What's that?' Everyone else was watching us now.

'No. I am a journalist. I am not here to wash cars.'

'Fair enough. I think you're right myself. The junior always washes the editor's car but you're right; it's time someone stood up to him.'

I carried on working on the fillers. 'How are we going to do this?' asked Jim.

'What?'

'How are we going to manage this revolt with least damage?'

Rick, Paddy and Stephen grinned widely.

'It's a tricky one,' said Stephen. 'We had this problem in Saskatchewan. You always get a couple sacked before the bosses relent. They have to draw blood. It's not often that you get someone as brave as Malachi in the front line.'

'I think', said Jim, 'I had better talk to Sean.'

Sean, the managing editor, had an adjacent office, down a short flight of stairs. He was an amiable but emphatic man. I'm not sure what he actually did. All I knew was that he was senior to Jim. He liaised with the cartoonist and many of the freelance contributors. I don't know why Pat didn't do that; perhaps because Pat was too important to do anything.

Jim went to talk to Sean.

Sean sent for me.

'What's your problem, Malachi?'

'I'm refusing to wash Pat's car.'

'Ah. You have thought this through?'

'It's a matter of principle, Sean.'

'I understand, but it has always been the custom here. The junior washes Pat's car. I did it myself before I was promoted. But I see your point and I wish maybe that I'd had the courage to take a stand like this myself.'

'I am a journalist, not a car washer. What would the union say about this?'

'Look, let me talk to Pat first and see if I can negotiate something.'

I went back to my desk and blushed red but tried to concentrate on the cuttings.

'I think you're dead right,' said Stephen.

'I don't know,' said Paddy. 'You don't want to throw away your job at this stage. You can't always pick the issues you stand on principle over. I would just wash the fucking car, Malachi.'

'What exactly is your objection?' said Rick.

'I am employed as a journalist, not a car washer.'

'But you're going to be paid a journalist's wage to do a car washer's job. A lot of people would think that was a good deal.'

'Well, I don't.'

'You'd rather wash a car for half the money?'

'I'm not going to wash a car.'

'Malachi, you are going to wash a lot of cars in the years to come. We all wash cars, until we're on top like Pat and we can tell someone else to do it for us. You wash your car, don't you, Jim?'

'If he thinks he's too good to wash a car, that's his business.'

'Yes, but every decision has its consequences. Is he ready for those consequences?'

'I am not going to wash his fucking car.'

So we all sat with our heads down, getting on with our

work, waiting for the next move.

Sean came up.

'Pat's ready to see you now.'

'Good luck,' said Jim. Eddie was grinning.

I walked up the ramp to Pat's door and knocked. Pat and Gwen stood looking at me, waiting for me to speak: Pat with his oiled hair brushed back, and Gwen, his secretary, blonde and groomed, with fresh lipstick on.

'Yes?' said Pat.

'I have come to tell you that —'

My tone was apologetic defiance, but Pat wasn't very good at this. Or perhaps he had more mercy. Before I had finished, he broke into a laugh. What did it mean? Did it mean he wasn't going to insist that I wash his car after all? That he admired my pluck? It was the first time I had seen him laugh. It was an affectionate laugh. Yes, I knew what it meant; it meant that I was a fool but that he liked me anyway.

'Thank you,' I said and turned and walked down the ramp.

They were all howling with laughter.

It was Jim's best sting yet.

'Bastards.'

'Don't take the bait,' said Rick. 'How many times do you have to be told?'

# Chapter 9

'You were supposed to have a by-line on that story', Jim told me. 'But they can't bear to have a Catholic name in this paper.' I'd been thinking the same thing myself.

When I had started on *The Sunday News*, there had been only two reporters, Jim and Paddy. Eddie started on the same day as me; that made four. Rick joined a week later, then Stephen. Now there was also a part-time reporter, another Canadian, called Susan. With the increased number of writers, the paper was starting to put by-lines on stories again. There is nothing worse than seeing the same by-line everywhere in a paper, but with six reporters, you can show off your talent.

My first by-line was on a story about Ballymurphy Enterprises, a project inspired by the controversial priest Des Wilson. It had been strange visiting a priest as a reporter. He had assumed that I was a stricken parishioner seeking advice or absolution. The name on my story was Mal O'Doherty. I assumed that this was a dilution of my Irishness to spare Protestant readers the shock of a full Catholic Irish name.

Now a story which Jim had instructed should carry a by-line had appeared without one. It was a large feature about the work of the Simon Community in North Belfast, the first of several stories that Jim got me to do about alcoholics. Others joked that it was his way of telling me that I was drinking too much, and perhaps it was. Either the sub-editor had ignored Jim's instruction or Jim had been overruled from above. Or possibly a compositor upstairs, laying out the flatbed type on the stone, had removed my name on his own initiative. Sometimes he would have to tighten lines to make things fit. He wasn't supposed actually to remove text.

I didn't care. I didn't want to engage in a sectarian quarrel, even from the position of being in the right. It also felt like vanity to insist on a by-line. I was going up to Andersonstown to follow up another story and on my way I dropped in at home. I was upstairs when there was a call at the door. My mother was settling Jim and Stephen in the living room when I came down.

'What's all this?'

'Pat wants you back in the office', said Jim. 'He's in a flap about you losing your by-line.'

Jim wasn't anxious — just amused — so neither was I. A working day had been turned into something like a holiday with the three of us driving down the Falls Road, talking office politics rather than work. Jim said: 'Pat wants to stamp out any suggestion that you are being discriminated against because of your name.'

'Am I not?'

'Certainly. I said you were to have your by-line. It's my job to make that decision.'

It sounded serious but also farcical. It had never occurred to me that anyone above me on the paper cared much about my sensibilities. I assumed that the capitalist system was ruthless and bigoted too and didn't have to care what I thought of it.

'What's the worst thing that can happen, Jim?'

'You can lose the rag.'

'I've no intention of losing the rag.'

'Then let him say whatever he is going to say.'

When we were seated in hushed and fearful expectancy in the editor's sanctum and Gwen had withdrawn to let the men prepare for battle, Pat started his speech. 'I want to reassure you all that there is no discrimination against Catholic names in this paper. Remarks have been made in the open office to suggest a policy of discrimination which — I have to tell you — does not exist and would not be tolerated.'

Leslie, the sub-editor, nodded. He had presumably told Pat what Jim had said. That's what had started this off. This meant we could not speak freely in the main office. That was worse than being right about discrimination. So long as we could vent our feelings and fears — even unfounded ones — no tension would build up. I didn't like this and I didn't know what to do or say. Was I expected to say something? Was this a challenge? I was too inexperienced to know what to say or to anticipate what Pat's fears might be. I can guess better now. I might have walked out and taken a job on *The Irish News* and written a story about how Century Newspapers discriminated against Catholics. I might have gone to the union. I might have raised a noisy complaint that would have further provoked the secret sectarian assertion which had cut my name from the paper. I might have given someone the fight he was looking for. I might have prolonged a quarrel that would have got nasty. Or I might simply have assented to being defined as the token taig who was best not getting above himself. Pat, I am sure, could see all that. All I could see was that he was going to disproportionate trouble to reassure me that something that had happened had not happened and, anyway, would not happen again.

The next by-line I got was for a story about students at Magee College in Derry protesting against the failure of the Vice-Chancellor of the University of Ulster to develop facilities there. Again I was Mal O'Doherty. This was clearly to be the compromise between the unpalatability of my full name and the danger of being accused of discriminating against me when leaving it out altogether.

There was an anarchic and mischievous spirit in the office. I wonder if this was our own compensation for the essential falseness of the world we created in print. Jim and I were the emotional ones. Paddy and Stephen had a sense of humour and sat marvelling sometimes at our extravagant interactions. Rick and Eddie were more withdrawn. They came to work to earn their pay, not to form bonds with other men in which they would expose their childish side.

We were typing on old clumpy machines, some of which were easier to use than others. There was no uniformity among them. Some were of the old black 'sit-up-and-beg' style. Some were curvier, big Imperials and Remingtons whose keys needed a good batter all the same, especially since we had to type onto three sheets at a time, with two sheets of carbon paper between them. We had no electric typewriters. They were not common yet and perhaps the rugged journalists of Jim's type would not have wanted them. I could certainly have worked faster on my own portable but I never thought of bringing it in. It wouldn't have lasted long under the rain of spilled tea and cigarette ash.

'Fuck it!' Jim was getting annoyed with his typewriter. We laughed at him, so he took the joke further and smashed his fist down into the keys, bunching them up. Again we laughed so he took his attack further still. He lifted the heavy machine, set it on the floor, and kicked it. Then he picked up a length of wood, left behind by some workmen, and thrust it into the keys.

'The crap they give us to work with.'

He sat down and called a maintenance office. 'We have a typewriter here that's in need of repair…. Yes, as soon as you can. Thank you.'

Venting frustration or just showing off? I'm not sure.

Stephen's fixation was with an American war plane. When he was doing nothing, just waiting for someone to call back, he would sit and carefully draw the outlines of the F4 Phantom. He would go into such close detail in his study of the F4 that he would not be able to finish his book on it. His first chapter would be longer than the whole book ought to be.

Often when he was drunk, Jim would say: 'What you or I do counts for nothing. We could vanish from the face of the earth and this paper would still come out on time. There will always be something to fill it with.'

Rick and Eddie were more restrained and conscientious. They did smile at these antics, but they would not have initiated anything disruptive. Once a senior member of staff passed through the office after a bomb scare and noticed that Jim had stayed at his desk and ignored the evacuation. Jim was suddenly the scolded junior as the man roared at him: 'Do you think this is some kind of joke? Do you think if a bomb goes off in here, it will spare you?'

One of the things that might have been playing in that man's mind was the fear that Jim, as a reporter and a nationalist, might indeed know more than himself about the real prospect of our being bombed. The man was hopping with anger. This wasn't someone who coped through black humour and blasé manners. For him, this was deadly serious and it darkened his days.

Jim or I or someone else might come into the office some morning with a hangover and expect not to be put under any pressure. Paddy's marriage was breaking up. He was allowed to sit morosely over the plans of the entertainment pages and to say nothing. One day, I taunted him and he lashed out with his fist, hit me in the ribs and hurled me winded across the room. Then he got his apology in first before I had the breath to voice mine. A system which depended on our being alert, co-operative and efficient would not have worked. We could not have done what the IRA and the loyalist UDA did, with the efficiency with which they did it.

The fear of death and imprisonment did not debilitate or hamper these people in the way that it hampered me and made me miserable: it gave them direction and energy.

*The Sunday News*, perhaps like most papers, was oblivious to process and pattern, even pattern that is plain to readers flicking now through the old files. News is incident after all. We looked into the miasma of political chaos, not for the thread that would explain it, but just for intriguing elements. What guns did the snipers use? That interested us. Where would the need for more and better guns take them? That did not.

Another couple of people making bombs blow themselves up: that's a story. That half of all IRA deaths were own goals at that time, no one seemed to notice. How will this affect recruitment or the bombing campaign itself? We had no idea. Would the IRA campaign die out after enough volunteers had simply been killed, or was there some process generating further interest among the young? Someone should have been wrestling with that question.

It was an embarrassing question for me. Why had I not joined the IRA myself, when so many of my neighbours had? Because I had not been beaten up by the army? I had. Because I not faced the humiliation of being a Catholic second-class citizen? I had. Because I was temperamentally averse to violence — and that perhaps because I was not very good at it? Well, that had to be part of the answer. Because I understood my political history better than those who did join up? Not really. I didn't understand it half as well as I thought I did.

Because I had sought a mentor and master not in a local paramilitary commanding officer but in a temperamental and cynical journalist? Perhaps that was it.

# Chapter 10

I was drinking in Kelly's one afternoon. This was my routine on a Saturday, to have a few pints in light-hearted company and then go to work. I would walk round to the *Sunday News* office in Donegall Street at about six. Walking through Belfast city centre at that time could be unnerving. Who knew what the IRA had planned for the city that night or whether a nervous soldier would shoot at a solitary stranger? But I faced the evening's work with the same levity. I never had much to do on a Saturday night.

As the junior reporter, I was not given the more important stories to handle, but I would sometimes be asked to accompany one of the older reporters, usually Stephen or Paddy, on a job. One night, Paddy, Rick and I went to the Unity Flats, having heard that there had been trouble there. We walked around the area in the dark and saw nothing. Then a group of soldiers asked us to go back towards North Street. This was not a regular foot patrol, but officers walking together, discussing some problem.

Paddy asked them why we should have to leave.

'Just do as I ask you,' said one of them. 'We have enough on our minds.'

'We're journalists,' I said, producing my new press card.

Paddy said: 'It's not for you to tell me where I can walk in my home town.'

Uh oh! I had seen this attitude often and it alarmed me. I felt it myself but I would not have asserted it so strongly. Other people, including my mother, had refused to be diverted away from gun battles. They insisted on living life by normal rules. Many people felt that if they didn't do that, they conceded a victory to the gunmen. The soldier drew a pistol and pointed it directly at Paddy's chest. 'Now fuck off or you'll get shot.'

'Come on, Paddy,' said Rick.

We turned away with big Paddy scowling back at them. 'There's press officers up in Lisburn getting eighty quid a week to pretend that you people are civilised. A waste of fucking money.'

This particular night, Jim and Eddie were at the office already. The old radio was crackling on the police frequency. In the middle of the night, I would hear that sound still rasping in my brain. I sat and read the morning papers again. I found a few small jobs to do, just to keep myself busy or at least looking busy. After a couple of hours, I stopped even doing that. I was reading *Playboy*. We heard a bomb explode in the distance. 'That's the start of it,' said Jim.

After a while, we would each, in turn, get a break, and, on mine, I would go down to the Duke of York for a pint and fetch fish suppers for the rest of them.

'See if you can get any word on the bomb,' Jim said that night.

I would call the army press office every hour anyway. The press officer told me that a bomb had gone off in a pub on North Queen Street. It wasn't far from us. Stephen and Paddy were out on another story, an interview with someone who claimed to have been beaten up by soldiers and had bruises to prove it. Their route back to the office took them past

McGurk's Bar which looked now just like a pile of rubble that had been dumped from a lorry. Jim took a call from them and told them he would join them later. 'Malachi, away and get me a packet of fags, would you, if you're going down to the Duke's.'

'Can I not go up to the bomb?'

'Do you know the area?'

'No.'

'Then you're not going.'

We had this ritual between us now that he would honour my professional status by not actually instructing me to do menial things, merely sounding me out on whether or not I was of a mind to do him a favour. I went for his fags. The bar was filling up. There were other journalists there watching the news on television, the first reports of the explosion at McGurk's bar. 'Looks like there's a few dead in this one,' said one of the reporters coming off the phone and giving another his turn. Some would go out to the scene. Others would manage to cover the whole thing well enough from their stools. 'Who has Jim sent?'

'Paddy and Stephen were already up there.'

Back upstairs in the office, we simply bided our time. There was an increased sense of urgency about the bomb. Jim was taking calls from news desks in London, asking his advice on the strength of the story. There is no way to make these things unfold any faster. We would go to press at about midnight. Most journalists twitch with urgency around a story like this. Jim did. He liked the performance. He was always half-acting, yet he was a brilliant reporter; he was acting the part of what he already was. I have known other journalists like that. Perhaps I do it myself sometimes. Jim liked talking down the phone with the feigned urgency of a broadcast correspondent.

The phone rang.

'How is it, Paddy?'

Paddy told me it was bad. Normally a bad bomb killed two or three people and many bombs killed nobody at all. There was also some gunfire, he said. Someone was shooting at the soldiers. I handed him over to Jim. Jim told him to come back and let Stephen stay on. Paddy brought Stephen's notes with him. Stephen stayed to help pull the rubble off the bodies.

I have learnt more about the bombing of McGurk's Bar in the years since than I learnt on the night itself. The pressure for me was just in waiting for news, wondering how I could help, taking notes from Paddy, Stephen and Jim which they could write into a front-page story later. They came back looking grim and intent on the story. After they had each written their share, Stephen went out, sat on the stairs and wept. We went to press with the story that ten had died. We were stretching it a bit; only eight bodies had yet been found. My brother Brian opened the door to me when I got home. I showed him the paper, expecting to shock him.

'I know. We've been watching it on telly.' That made me wonder again what all Paddy and Stephen's risk and effort had been for.

Jim must have stayed on to update the story. A late edition reports that by 3 a.m. fourteen bodies had been recovered, though none had been identified, at least to the press. In one of his familiar misspellings, he wrote that the 'death tole' mounted as the hours passed. We reported that an army major, two policemen and at least two civilians had been shot when gunmen 'sprayed the area with automatic fire following a confrontation between Catholic and Protestant crowds'.

An extension of the story on page 3 described McGurk's as 'known to have been regularly frequented by members and supporters of the Republican movement.' Though the story is carefully written to avoid attributing the bomb or the gunshots to one side or the other, this complies with two versions that developed later: one, that the bomb was made by the IRA and went off accidentally, and another that loyalists had attacked the bar to kill republicans. Both stories were wrong. The account given in *Lost Lives*, a collation of the dead, edited by David McKittrick, says that McGurk's was bombed by the UVF but that it had not been their first choice of target that night. It was a bar frequented by Catholics, with no particular republican character to it. It was bombed by loyalists who did not want to take their bomb back home with them, having failed in their mission.

A friend who was once a loyalist says, 'You know, a lot of sectarianism was just laziness; people who weren't ordered to kill random Catholics would do it because it was easier.'

McGurk's was a family bar. Philomena, the mother, and 14-year-old Maria, who lived there, would be among the dead. The final toll was 15 dead from the explosion and one soldier shot dead. Of the dead in the bar, eight suffocated in the rubble. Initially we believed that the bomb had exploded inside the bar. Jim himself later told me that an IRA man was punished for not collecting the bomb. That was what the gossip said. Terrorism experts later wrote that the IRA had been training others in the construction of a bomb when it had gone off. That explained, they said, the clustering of the bodies inside the bar; they had all been leaning over the gelignite to see how it was detonated. That was an image that fitted in with the smug officer-class assumption that the Irish were stupid.

Many people believed that the carnage in McGurk's was an 'own goal', and this was plausible because so many IRA bombers were dying in accidents at the time.

Dr William Rutherford was the head of Casualty at the Royal Victoria Hospital. On that night, he later told me, he moved the whole unit up to the bar to treat the injuries. 'I brought morphine to treat the pain, but we didn't need it. People were in such shock that they felt nothing. I had never seen that before.'

A police officer has told me that his father brought him into the hospital to see the injured, to impress upon him the damage that political violence was doing. One of the survivors, John McGurk, became a journalist in Belfast himself. John grieves that his family got little sympathy because the bombing was reported, even years later, as an IRA own goal.

Lord Gerry Fitt later told the House of Lords, in a debate on the Good Friday Agreement, that he had pulled bodies from the wreckage and that one had come apart in his hands.

Inside the paper that week, however, we had nearly as much copy about the war between India and Pakistan as we had about our own troubles. We had a story that the Civil Rights Association was planning mass protests against internment in the new year. That edition also carried my story about Jimmy Smith, the otter hunter of the River Finn, the 'hero of local fishermen'. Jimmy was selling the pelts for £5 each. 'I look for the tracks of the otter in the gravel at the bed of the river and follow them upstream.'

This is another example of a story that would be handled differently today, but even then one reader was outraged: 'Otters have as much right to the fish as he and his fishermen friends have as it is their natural food,' wrote (Mrs) Alison Gregg of Finaghy Road North. 'I know I am not alone in my condemnation of this man's revolting hobby.'

Another story in that issue that would be handled differently today reported an assault on two young girls.

> Two young girls about 11 years old were attacked and stripped by a mob of youths just outside the city boundary last night. The girls were in Rosapenna Street near the Oldpark area when the youths surrounded them. After being stripped completely, their clothes were burned in the street and they were then abandoned.

That's the sort of story that would make tabloid front pages today and feature on the main television news. Then, it was left unfinished. Most readers must have wanted to know if this was a sectarian attack and, if so, whether the girls were Catholics or Protestants. Or was it a punishment attack by the junior wing of a paramilitary group against two girls who had been friendly with soldiers or policemen or with Catholics or Protestants? Or perhaps it was simply an indecent assault. We were not told and the paper did not speculate.

The next Saturday night's bomb, on the Shankill Road, killing two small children and two adults, was probably the IRA's retaliation for the bombing of McGurk's. If no one else believed that the IRA had not left a bomb in McGurk's Bar, they at least knew it themselves.

A 15-year-old boy watched a green car deliver this bomb. The car pulled up outside the Balmoral Furniture Store. A man got out and set the bomb on the doorstep. The blast caused the building to collapse, killing Harold King, an auctioneer's assistant and, ironically, a Catholic. A mother pushing a pram suffered a shower of rubble. Two-year-old Tracey Munn was killed. Others to die were 17-month-old Colin Nicholl and the doorman, Hugh Brice. Local men beat up a Protestant man for a comment that led them to mistake him for a Catholic. A picture we used became one of the iconic images of that period. It showed a fireman carrying a dead baby wrapped in a blanket; it spoke of the futility and simple lack of focus of the competing bombing campaigns.

If the newspaper was one attempt to interpret what was going on — and a poor one — another was the stock of lore exchanged by journalists and others. This account was not for printing and not confined by the law.

A group of us might be in a cubicle in Kelly's exchanging yarns. Here is one of Jim's: 'There is this sniper up in Derry called McGuinness. He's got nerves of steel. He was out operating one night and the Brits thought they had him surrounded. McGuinness jumps over a wall with his rifle in his hand and he's in combats and it's dark and he finds himself right in the lap of an army patrol. And they're all crouched down, crapping themselves. And McGuinness realises he has one chance. He bolts upright and salutes: Sah! And they take him for one of their own. "Keep your fuckin' head down, lad," says the officer. "McGuinness is out there."'

Some of these stories were put about by political activists. They were propaganda. Others were just the fantasies of people trying to make sense of chaos. For a journalist, stories that showed an intimate knowledge of the IRA and an acquaintance with the members were proof of credibility.

In the same issue in which we reported the bombing of McGurk's Bar, we carried a story about Gerry O'Hare, just released from internment and seeking a court order to have his wife Rita moved from prison to hospital. Rita was recovering from the bullets that had struck her during an ambush on a British army patrol. She had bullet wounds to her head, neck and side, and Gerry said that she was not being given proper care. One day, when she was brought to Belfast for a bail hearing, prison officers left her alone for hours in a cell. I couldn't see the average *Sunday News* reader caring much.

What we knew about her husband was that he was the press officer for the first Battalion of the Provisional IRA. Could we have included that detail in our story? Would it have been relevant? Perhaps our readers would have formed their own opinions about him anyway.

Most people had secrets in those days. There would be long political discussions in the bar, but what did you really know about some of the people in your company? The girls whom you were hoping to get closer to might be friends of a prisoner or a man on the run. They might even be members of the intelligence section of the IRA or Cumann na mBan, or they might just be excited by the new atmosphere in the city, the sense that a revolution was under way. I'm thinking of times when I would be trying to impress a girl with stories about journalism and I would see a wee knowing look in her eye. Every man sees that, or ought to, when he has betrayed his ignorance. In those days, it also came at the point at which she had worked out that you knew less about the machinations of political movements and armed groups than she did herself. It wasn't enough to impress her just with accounts of bullets flying over your head or being beaten up by the army; everyone had yarns like that.

*The Sunday News* liked to have stories which countered the easy assumptions about the troubles; not deep analytical pieces, but quirky side views of things that told you that the man behind the mask thought and reacted like a human being, got married, missed his wife. It never went so far as to challenge readers to, for instance, consider that the IRA had a just point; the paper wouldn't have done that. It maintained a relationship with the police and the army through trite little stories about the RUC advising people to exercise their own discretion in dealing with vigilantes or not to 'have a go' at gunmen.

Among the better stories were those that provided a lateral slant on events. An example was a story about a Free Presbyterian minister, just released from jail, who claimed that most Catholics detained under the Special Powers Act, on suspicion of being members of the IRA, were not in the IRA at all but were being converted to militancy by their treatment in prison. The Rev. William McCrea said: 'It would be naïve to think that being subjected to detention and interrogation will not engender deep hatred in these men for the rest of their lives and this hatred could well be passed on to their children.'

That showed up a rare concurrence between the view of many liberal social observers and that of an evangelical fundamentalist. Thirty-odd years later, McCrea is still a sidekick of the Rev. Ian Paisley, and has never been regarded as sympathetic to the IRA or the Catholic community. Far from it. So this disclosure, of his understanding of how the abuse of innocents turned them against the state, glows like a gem of simple but rare sanity. Of course, its value to McCrea was not in its patent wisdom but in its reinforcing his political argument that the Stormont government had botched the war against the IRA and was making things worse.

More representative of the smug Protestant take on the troubles was a letter in the same edition from 'New Ulster Cynic', hankering after the days when 'we all lived in peace' before troublemakers wrecked the harmonious balance of a well-governed society: 'Perhaps the greatest paradox is the association which calls itself Civil Rights. Isn't it strange how we were all able to live our lives happily (even if some politicians did not have the power they coveted) until that Association defied the law and bestowed upon us, by divine right, street politics and took from us all the right to peace and laughter.'

# Chapter 11

It was winter and it was grim and we seemed to spend much of it in traffic jams because of either bomb scares or roadblocks set up to search our cars. The army might be looking for IRA men on the run; they might be checking that all passengers were travelling willingly and were not being taken off to a back alley or country road to be shot in the head. The IRA was proving its skills by springing members from jail. Tucker Kane and Tommy Gorman led an operation to release their OC, Sean Convery, from Crumlin Road prison in November 1971. Tommy Gorman has told me about it.

'First of all, Tucker Kane and I reconnoitred behind the jail, wearing overalls. When approached, we said we were from the council, checking for vermin.'

A local man insisted they come into his house and check the dampness of the walls. To keep their cover, they went along with this and took notes. Gorman and Kane were worried about a lookout post on the prison wall. Because of the webbing over it, they could not make out if anyone was in it. So, on the day of the break-out, they sent two women into the street, posing as Avon ladies. The two were wearing scant miniskirts, to give the soldiers, if they were in the lookout, something to concentrate on.

'There was no movement from the box so there was either nobody in it or they were too engrossed in the two women in the miniskirts to see us. We threw the rope ladders over and Tucker Kane went up and sat on the wall with a submachine gun to frighten any screws off. There was a football match on in the yard. They all stampeded towards the wall. Convery was trampled and didn't get out. Nine others did. I took four of them in the car,' Gorman says.

They had brought ten cars with them for escaping prisoners.

One night in the Old House, gossip went round that three more IRA men had escaped from the Crumlin Road prison. That cheered everybody up. I was there with Maguire and marvelling at the unattainably beautiful Rose McCartney singing 'Four Green Fields'. On the way home, a patrol stopped us and checked our names. One of the escaped IRA men was called Doherty, so the private taking my details rushed back to his officer with the news that he had an O'Doherty. The officer shrugged. He was probably saying: 'You should do a week in Derry; they're all called Doherty up there.'

The coverage of the escape said something about the different press perspectives on the IRA. *The Sunday News* couldn't resist a joke — a cartoon by Martyn Turner showing a winding traffic jam, with the line: 'I don't see why, if three prisoners escaped down the Crumlin Road on a Thursday afternoon, we have to serve their sentence on the Sydenham bypass on a Friday morning.'

We laughed a lot at the mischief of the militants. There was a long-established lore of marvelling at their antics which went back to the nineteenth century at least. Hadn't we all read stories about Dan Breen and Michael Collins making the whole British state ridiculous by walking through roadblocks set up to catch them? It was a cliché, and Doherty,

Meehan and McCann, doing the same thing, placed themselves in the longer history of republican mischief-making and even in a sense legitimised the Provos. Now there would be new rebel songs about the people of the 1970s, establishing that this current campaign was not an aberration or a flash of madness but a recurrence of history. And if the songs and the yarns affirmed that we were reliving our past, that made the case that the problem was not our fixation on violence and related antics; the problem was the British.

Christmas was coming and the IRA — great lads that they were — wrecked the transport service by burning buses, and jammed the traffic in the town with bombs and bomb scares. It was further propaganda of the deed, using minimal resources to impress the largest possible number of people with the message that Northern Ireland was ungovernable.

One of Jim's regular contacts at that time was Chris, a PR man for a brewery. Chris was a bright and witty man of 24, whose job was to entertain journalists in the hope that they would write well about beer — hardly too much to ask of most journalists. On our last Saturday night before Christmas, he brought a barrel of beer into the office and we had a party.

In the taxi home, I looked out at the darkened Falls Road. The crouching paratroopers with blackened faces followed us through their gun-sights. I had already worked out that they could shoot on any notion that took them and that the army would cover for them, as it had covered for the men who shot the two women, Meehan and Maguire. They could say that a man in the car had pointed a gun at them, that they had shot him in self-defence and that a crowd had gathered and taken the gun away. They did not shoot that night at this lone car on the dark road at two in the morning. Too much paperwork afterwards, I suspect.

On Christmas Day, Civil Rights marchers walked along the

motorway past our home, to the Long Kesh prison camp, to protest against internment, and, I presume, lift the spirit of the prisoners. I watched from below the bridge and momentarily thought of running up the embankment and joining them — for the crack!

# Part Three

# Chapter 12

*The Sunday News* faced optimistically into 1972. The front page of the 2 January edition carried a series of predictions by 'world-renowned clairvoyant' Maurice Woodruff, 'who has the uncanny gift of seeing events to come.' Mr Woodruff was presented not as a man who claimed to have such powers but simply as one who actually had them. He is more famous now for having advised Peter Sellers on what roles to take than for reading the future of Northern Ireland, and he is played by Stephen Fry in *The Life and Death of Peter Sellers*.

Woodruff's predictions related to the prospects facing leading political figures. 'For Mr Brian Faulkner Mr Woodruff sees a favourable start to the New Year with the PM being able to relax by March because the violence will have abated.' Actually, by March, Faulkner would indeed feel his workload ease, since the government at Westminster would prorogue the Stormont parliament of which he was Prime Minister and appoint a Secretary of State, William Whitelaw, to govern Northern Ireland directly.

There was a prediction also for one of the leaders of the Provisional IRA: 'During 1972, Provisional IRA leader Mr Joe Cahill will be persuaded by public opinion how unpopular his methods of achieving his aims have become.' He would not. The coming year was to be the worst of the whole troubles. The IRA demonstrated its coherence and discipline with a two-week ceasefire in July, negotiated directly with the British government and barricaded several areas of Belfast and Derry against the security forces.

Inside the same edition, there was a full page of this reassuring nonsense: 'All the indications are that it would take a great deal to satisfy Mr Hume [the deputy leader and chief strategist of the SDLP] and that he does not have the most satisfactory year ahead for him because he will allow himself to be overruled by fanatical people in his public life.' There was something in that. Hume was to mediate between the IRA and the British government and help the paramilitaries to win effective political status for prisoners, but his efforts to persuade the IRA to wrap up its campaign were to fail.

Ted Heath, the British Prime Minister, 'will announce his engagement to marry towards year's end.' That didn't happen either. He would be a bachelor all his days.

Dr Ian Paisley 'is a man of God. He is also a man of principle. During 1972 his whole outlook will change and he will start to think of the people and the country as a whole.' True — in a way. After the proroguing of Stormont, Paisley campaigned, for a time, for the full integration of Northern Ireland into the UK.

This stuff was written halfway between the bombing of McGurk's Bar and Bloody Sunday at the end of that month. Yet another prophecy that didn't come true was one in an inside-page story that said that fresh food would no longer be available by the year 2000. 'Hoteliers and restaurant managers claim that to prepare a complete menu of fresh food is virtually impossible.'

Another story reported the marriage of an internee, for a

readership which included people who did not dismiss them all as evil terrorists.

> Mary Barr is probably the loneliest bride in Britain ... for a few hours after her wedding ceremony last week her husband Alexander bade her farewell and walked sadly back behind the drab barbed wire fences of Long Kesh internment centre.

The picture shows Mary looking sadly at her wedding photograph. There is a hint below that the compositors were not happy with the story. Someone had jumbled the type of the first paragraph to reorder the lines and make nonsense of them.

And, of course, there was all the other news. George Best was going out with 19-year-old Miss Great Britain, Carolyn Moore, though she was denying that they had plans to marry. The caption under a picture of George said: 'Soccer star George Best was back at his home in Bramhall, Cheshire, last night but he would not speak about his problems. He answered the phone to a reporter but hung up when he was asked what time he had arrived home.'

The coy tone of the paper suggested that the moral worth of a man is judged by the time he gets to bed.

It was in early January that I interviewed the eccentric Ulster Constitution Party councillor Robert Lindsay Mason, who had just recently been elected unopposed in the Falls ward, since nationalist politicians were abstaining from local government in protest against internment. My story said that he was treading warily. It quoted him saying: 'I think going into the Falls at the present time would be very foolish. I am sure there are a few trigger-happy republicans in there and I don't want to take the risk of being a handy target for one of them.'

The first time Robert Lindsay Mason set foot on the Falls Road was when he was invited there to pose for our photographer. When I had phoned him to ask if he might subject himself to the risk of being photographed in the ward he had been elected to represent, I heard him call out for permission: 'Mummy?'

# Chapter 13

A week before Bloody Sunday, reporters found themselves out on Magilligan Strand, covering a Civil Rights riot, the messiest yet. The marchers had tried to walk along the beach on a January Saturday to reach the prison where several internees were being held. This was in line with the new back-to-the-streets policy we had predicted in the paper. The march from Belfast to Long Kesh on Christmas Day had been peaceful. This one was a shambles.

> The clashes came on the beach. Marchers — singing, jeering and some linking arms — tried to round the barbed wire fence leading from the camp to the beach and rocks. The tide was low and the demonstrators tried to march through the gap between the end of the fence and the waterline.
>
> Two hundred troops from the first Battalion of the Parachute Regiment and the second Battalion, the Royal Green Jackets — backed by police who were on duty — fired rubber bullets at point-blank range into the crowd and then drove them back in a baton charge.

Jim observed: 'I wouldn't much fancy trying to tell one of those guys that I was a reporter.'

Reporters like to have a clearly demarcated space at the side of a riot, where both sides can see that they are not participants. But what would you do if you found yourself in a situation where hundreds of marchers were being scattered: stand passively aside and affect professional detachment, hoping that no rampaging soldier would hit you over the head with a baton?

There were intimations before the Bloody Sunday march the following week that it would meet with resistance. *The Sunday News* reported on the morning of 31 January that civil rights leaders had confirmed that they were going ahead with their illegal march in Derry. But a planned loyalist counter-protest had been called off. The paper quoted the vice-chairman of the Derry Democratic Unionist Party, the Rev. James McClelland: 'We believe wholesale riot and bloodshed could be the result of the civil rights activities tomorrow and we would be held responsible if our rally takes place. We have also appealed to all loyalists to stay out of the city centre tomorrow.'

I was at home watching television when the first newsflash said that paratroopers had opened fire on the parade in Derry. Throughout the course of the afternoon, the figure for the dead rose from two to eight to 11 to 13. This was heart-sickening to contemplate. It confirmed how easy it might be to die, how readily some people would kill you. I dwelt on this. I dwelt on the injustice of sudden unwarranted death.

On the evening news came the claims that the Paras had run amok and fired on unarmed protesters. Outside, on the main Andersonstown Road, we heard the first blast bombs and the whoops and yells of a gleeful crowd. Sometimes it is more unnerving, if safer, to sit in your home and stay away from the danger; but then you have either to shut out the sounds or to make sense of them. Suddenly there was a storm of popping, like dozens of small pistols firing together. It was the food cans exploding in the heat of the fire of the Busy Bee supermarket.

What scared me now was that the ceiling on what was thinkable was still rising. And yet, frightening as it was, there was carnival in it too, at least in Belfast. I went the next day to visit my friend Fegan and saw children tobogganing down the hill on convector heaters looted from a hijacked lorry. Teenagers were distributing stolen food around some of the houses.

That night, the Paras were back in Belfast. They carried themselves with pride. Some of them rested the rifle butt on the hip and walked with a pronounced swagger. I fantasised about shooting into their broad backs.

*The Sunday News* had not covered the story of the Bloody Sunday killings because they came too early in the week for us. Then we were hampered in how we might follow it up. Ted Heath immediately asked Lord Justice Widgery to conduct an inquiry. That made the whole story *sub judice*, or at least the media accepted that it did, without testing it. On the following Saturday night, I was writing a story. Sean had come in to make sure we stuck to the rules: 'No comment. No loaded language.'

'Can I use the word "massacre"?'

'No, you can't.'

'But what is the dictionary definition of massacre?'

'I don't fucking care.'

Yet though Sean was scrupulous in avoiding anything that might be regarded as *sub judice* in the text of our stories and articles, he was happy to publish a cartoon by Martyn Turner which questioned the integrity of Justice Widgery himself. The judge is seen in his wig and gown, holding up the scales of justice. In one pan there is the 'Bogside version' and in the other the 'Army version'. Ted Heath in the foreground explains: 'He must be impartial, he's English.'

Widgery, for his attempt to establish a historical record

that absolved the soldiers, so contradicted the popular view of what had happened that day that the contention never subsided. Though I didn't cover the massacre itself, I often, in later years, covered the commemoration parade and interviewed people who had been there, including Bishop Edward Daly and Denis Bradley.

A Derry comedian says: 'You know what the shock of Bloody Sunday was — we had imagined that the Brits would come in and recognise that we were not fuzzy wuzzies but were just the same as themselves. We assumed that they wouldn't shoot us, that they would behave better here than they had in Aden. But we were just mad paddies to the Paras. They didn't give a fuck about us. Seeing that was scary. It left people asking, who are we? We were just fuzzy wuzzies, after all.'

I had a deepening fear that there was no secure moral ground or right position to take in relation to the violence. I certainly would have been less critical of the murder of paratroopers after Bloody Sunday than of the murder of civilians, until a revenge attack on their barracks at Aldershot by the Official IRA killed seven civilians. You couldn't even have clean revenge; you had to put too much faith in murderous people and their callous and inept ways. The only just revenge would have been lightning bolts from the sky, incinerating the filthy hearts of those soldiers and sparing their cooks and chaplain. Such bolts don't come.

Another journalist who remembers that time is the poet Brian Lynch. In his *Pity for the Wicked*, he recalls the mood in the newsroom he worked in when reports of the bombing of Aldershot came in.

The day this news began to break
Our Foreign Sub banged down his fist
And roared: 'The Paratroops have got
Their answer now! A bomb has been

Put under them in Aldershot.
The roof's come down on their canteen!'
The newsroom rang with howls of joy.
They'd murdered us. We'd murdered them.
And I joined in, a roaring boy
Who cheered the Butcher's requiem.

# Chapter 14

Home life in Riverdale was as stressful as anything at work. Sometimes in the evening, sitting watching television with my mother, we would pass no comment between us but turn up the volume when shots were fired or a blast bomb was thrown nearby. Many of the women in those days were almost humming with stress and they were taking the addictive tranquillisers doctors prescribed liberally in those days: Valium and Librium.

When I did try to convey in the paper some of my private understanding of life in Andersonstown, I did it in disguise. Jim suggested a feature on the experience of a housewife in the area. This housewife would not be identified and could be a composite of two or more people. In the end, she was my own invention and a vehicle for detail about the life I watched around me. The commentary was more accurate than any I could have risked giving under my own name.

> Even in August 1969 we did not see much bother up here. But now life is miserable. A few weeks ago there was more trouble on the Andersonstown Road than I have ever seen before. Most of the shops in the area were burnt out and now we

have only half the supermarkets we had the week before Bloody Sunday. I don't use banks very often but I had a small savings account. Then all the banks in the area were destroyed. I was told that my account was transferred to a branch of the Savings Bank in King Street, but that has been bombed too. I don't know what I'm going to do about it now but that's the least of my worries....

The bus service in this part of town is awful. We understand the Corporation taking the buses off after so many were burnt out but where does that leave us? Until last week we had to take taxis. Sure there was a special service but we were packed in like sardines and charged three bob a trip. It was cheaper than usual but the drivers were making a fortune....

I hate going to the shops or moving very far from the house. Even during the day there are gun battles close by which are never mentioned in the papers. It hasn't happened to me yet but a neighbour of mine was only a few yards away when gunmen shot two policemen in a boutique near here. And another woman down the street was passing a bank when a gun battle broke out between IRA men coming out and police waiting on them. The whole street had to dive for cover.

Sometimes I'm hanging the washing out on the line when you hear a rattle of gunfire a few streets away and you know they have ambushed an army patrol.

The night can be worst of all. For a while we used to sit and listen to the bombs and the shooting. It got so that the kids could tell the difference between nail bombs and bigger bombs. And they used to pick out what type of guns were being used by the sound of the shots....

Now all we do is sit watching television and then go to bed. Some nights we cannot sleep because of the shooting. You wouldn't dare go out now. There are no lights in the street. Vandals have wrecked everything. You can hear them roaming about the streets outside. And if it isn't them it's the army. They have never been to our house but most homes in

> this district have been searched at some time or other. They burst in.
>
> I have seen them dragging the men away and the women and kids crying outside the house....
>
> It doesn't seem to affect some of the women who live in the streets around here. When the armoured cars roar in for a raid at night they jump out of bed and start banging bin lids and blowing whistles so that the boys on the run know to get out. At least four houses in this street put up men on the run. I have seen them but I never say anything ... it's best to pretend you don't see. I couldn't help men on the run. My nerves are bad enough as it is.

Though I comment here on how circumspect the paper was in its coverage of political violence, I was circumspect myself when given a chance to describe life in Riverdale. I was afraid of identifying, even inadvertently, the people who kept safe houses and those who stayed in them: Tucker Kane, Tommy Gorman and the others. I was afraid of these people but I also feared that if I disclosed too much familiarity with the ways of the IRA, I would attract the scrutiny of the police or even of the loyalist workers in the print room below.

Though I was only a few months now into my job at *The Sunday News*, and getting the hang of it, I was starting to think that I should leave Northern Ireland. This was, in one sense, a cowardly and selfish option and might, in another, be viewed as an act of self-preservation. If I didn't get killed, I might become so callous, cynical and angry that I would not be the same person anyway. Jim persuaded me that it would be easier to get another job as a reporter if I had a full year's experience before leaving.

Stephen's stories from his life in Canada and his travels in Mexico encouraged me.

'Just go,' he would say.

'But a time may be coming when I will be needed here,

when I might have to get a gun and defend my family home. Is the army going to do it?'

'Malachi, in a war you will be no fucking use to anybody.'

Stephen was under pressure from his parents to leave Northern Ireland too. There were times when gunfire near his home made him feel sick in his stomach. Often a sniper opened up on soldiers in his street. His twin baby daughters would sleep through the shooting and, from a bedroom window, he would watch the soldiers manoeuvre to outflank the sniper.

*The Sunday News* was a strange paper for Belfast, but it thrived. By 1972, its sales were double what they had been when it had started out: over 110,000 copies a week. They were high probably because it was the only local paper covering the Saturday-night bombings. Still, what need had anyone of news in print when it would already have come out on television?

The paper carried few political interviews and concentrated on fringe figures rather than on central operators. One of these interviews was with G.B. Newe, the Community Relations Minister at Stormont and 'the loneliest man in Ulster'. Newe told Stephen that, as a Catholic minister, he was able to mediate Catholic concerns to other government departments: 'It's been difficult for Catholics, remember, to talk to a minister of government in the past. But with me they can talk frankly.'

Stephen did not mention in his article that the SDLP was demanding that Newe resign and stop giving credibility to a government whose collapse the party was working for.

Another fringe figure Stephen interviewed was Armagh MP Jack McGinnis, presented as a novel liberal within unionism because he supported the demand for a Bill of Rights for Northern Ireland and a once-and-for-all referendum on the union with Britain. This liberal later featured in the paper as a stalwart of Ulster Vanguard, a militant loyalist organisation threatening a coup.

The paper was more interested in novelty than analysis of the core issues. We did not sit Prime Minister Brian Faulkner down and ask him how he hoped to restore stable government to Northern Ireland. Nor did we ask former Home Affairs Minister William Craig, the leader of Vanguard, how he would react if the British called his bluff about fighting for Ulster. Craig had been the hate figure of the Civil Rights movement because he had banned their parades. Now he was fallen from government and strutting around like Oswald Mosley, rallying loyal Ulstermen and inspecting them in militarised ranks. He was predicting that the British would abolish Stormont and that a time would come for Ulster Protestants to prepare to defend their homeland.

*The Sunday News* was more interested in the political debates in the local government councils than these murmurs of distant thunder. Why was this? I can think of several reasons. There were more stories in the councils and more novel stories there too. Robert Lindsay Mason, who needed permission from 'Mummy' to go into the Falls ward that he had been elected to represent, was a more interesting figure than Paisley or Craig. At least there was something surprising about him. He wasn't tied to the party line of a big party and the big parties were now only reacting to circumstances created by the militants.

Jim was more sympathetic to republicanism than unionism, and more to the left-wing Official republican movement than to the Provisionals, whom he regarded as Catholic chauvinists who would take us into a sectarian civil war. He also had good contacts among unionist councillors. His fancy was that the Protestant and Catholic working classes would unite in a revolution against Britain.

Trawling through the files of *The Sunday News* for that

year, you find hundreds of little stories that have been lost to the historical record, that aren't recycled in the books about that period, and which appeared in the paper, most often, simply because they happened on a Saturday. Other stories of monumental events, even on the doorstep of *The Sunday News*, like the Donegall Street bomb, are hardly mentioned because they happened on a weekday.

In February 1972, two weeks after Bloody Sunday, Derry IRA men brought a bomb to the Woodleigh Hotel on Asylum Road. There was a wedding reception on at the time. The bombers told the wedding guests that they had three minutes to get out. One of the unexpected duties of the best man, Phonsie Patton, was to plead with the bombers to go away and let them enjoy their party. The bombers shot him in the face.

The couple getting married that day were Dennis Patton from Eastway in Creggan and Tina Kelly from the Bogside. Well, at least the IRA wasn't being sectarian — it was ruining the lives of people from the housing estates from which it claimed allegiance.

Phonsie probably didn't understand that many IRA bombers had no access to the timer and would be blown up themselves if they didn't get away. Half the IRA men and women who died that year were killed by their own bombs, when they didn't get to the target on time.

# Chapter 15

The British government was making plans for us and these plans were leaking out. Some leaks came from the Labour Opposition, which was being briefed on the thinking of the Prime Minister, Ted Heath. Some were coming from the unionist constituency associations, which were being briefed by the Northern Ireland Prime Minister and Unionist Party leader, Brian Faulkner.

The British government presumably had no objection to these leaks and indeed may have seen them as a way of testing new political ideas on the Northern Ireland public. It was not just high-powered, London-based political columnists and analysts who were openly discussing proposals for the removal of the government of Northern Ireland; the *Sunday News* columnist John D. Stewart was among those who boasted of knowing Britain's plans.

After Bloody Sunday, the British signalled that they would seek to replace the government of Northern Ireland and release internees. What they were less explicit about was that they were also opening negotiations with the IRA to secure a truce. The IRA was as discreet about this as was the government. The British were hoping that the suspension of the Stormont parliament, when it came, would be sufficient to placate the two wings of the IRA without triggering an armed revolt among loyalists. This seemed a real danger with the rapid growth of loyalist militancy. Suddenly there were gangs all over Belfast which identified themselves by different tartan scarves. Rick did a story about these tartan gangs. The gang he met up with on a Belfast street was not the most fearsome but he did his best to make it sound as if it was. 'A wave of terror hit me as a flick knife flashed.'

The boys told Rick that they beat up any Catholics who passed through Protestant areas. Who had organised these gangs? What was their relationship with the paramilitaries? We don't learn anything about this from the article. The question doesn't arise, so the article stands as evidence not, as intended, of the spread of organised sectarian violence, but of the strange detachment of our newspaper, serving the moral outrage of people who were presumed to have little sense of how bad things really were.

One clue to how unreal this moral outrage was to the people in the most troubled areas was a quote at the end of the article from John McQuade, MP for Shankill. 'The [gangs] give protection to the police and army as much as the police and army give protection to the people in the area. The police have never complained to me about the gangs.'

The Dominican nun Sister Lucina recalls that when she was studying at Newtownabbey Tech in 1972, she learnt off a verse that another student had engraved on her desk. It went:

Give me oil in my lamps, keep them burning.
Give me tartan round my neck, I pray.
Give me bullets for my gun;
I will shoot them every one,
The fenians and the IRA.

Craig's Vanguard movement seemed then to be the most likely rallying force for unionist militancy. Craig would arrive at his rallies in an open-topped car, accompanied by motorbike outriders. His language was threatening. At a rally in Lisburn, he said that an evil conspiracy threatened the country's existence and 'God help those who get in our way for we mean business.' What Craig hoped to do was mimic the tactics that had worked for republicans in Dublin in 1919 and establish a provisional government. At least that was his declared aim. Craig wasn't the only faction leader promising more than he could deliver. The same issue of the paper reported that John Lennon and Yoko Ono were coming to live in Northern Ireland to help the campaign for civil rights.

Kevin McCorry of the Northern Ireland Civil Rights Association had told a reporter, probably Jim: 'All we know is that he is coming and when he arrives he will be accepting the discipline of CRA. He won't be working with any other organisation.' This was intended probably as a poke in the eye for the Provos, who were talking to Lennon too.

There were rumours at that time that Leon Uris was in town researching the novel that would become *Trinity*, and that different parties were competing for the opportunity to influence him, as well.

One thing that Catholics and Protestants from the Falls and the Shankill agreed on, according to the paper, was their opposition to a new ring road for Belfast to connect the M2 and the M1. 'Shankill and Falls Protest' said the headline, but the real story was that they would not protest together. James McWilliams of the 'Republican inspired Belfast Housing Action Group' threatened to obstruct the work because 'it would necessitate the building of high-rise houses, would perpetuate the religious ghettos and would do little to improve traffic conditions in the city in the long term.' These predictions were not borne out. No new high-rise buildings were created. The religious ghettos were perpetuated, but more credit for that must go to the paramilitaries themselves than to the road and, though Belfast is now congested with traffic, few, if any, would argue that removing the West Link would ease that congestion.

Jim's sympathies gave him access to republican activists. He was especially excited by the break-out from the prison ship *Maidstone*. This was another E Company operation involving Tucker Kane, Tommy Gorman, Sean Convery and others. Kane and Gorman had failed to spring Convery, their OC, from Crumlin Road Prison. Now that they were all interned together on the prison ship, they tried again. It was a complex and brilliant plan which entailed seducing a seal into the range of the security alarms around the ship to find a blind spot. The plan was that the men would mingle with shipyard workers at four o'clock and slip out among them. The IRA sent a lorry for them with dry clothes and hot soup. An end-of-day head-count of prisoners, however, was botched, so that moment was lost and the gang had to make its move later, after a second count.

The *Maidstone* break-out nearly failed. Seven IRA men, including Convery — who was not a good swimmer and nearly drowned — leapt from the ship into Belfast Lough one night in February and made their way to shore. Jim, my news editor, was in the Markets area where the two wings of the IRA, which usually bristled beside each other, co-operated in distracting the search parties with decoy fire. Tommy Gorman got off first and feared initially that he was the only one to have survived. He had heard Convery screaming to God in the water. Slowly the others came ashore, waddling like strange beasts, their arms lengthened into floppy tendrils by the socks they had worn to protect their hands against the hawser they had slid down. They got onto the shuttle bus for the workers and bullied the driver into taking them out. The men went to a bar in the Markets area. The customers in the bar gave them clothes. One even gave Tommy Gorman the keys to his car.

The main impact of the escape on me was that it freed Kane and Gorman back into Riverdale. They would make our corner a centre for IRA attacks against the army.

# Chapter 16

The Abercorn restaurant in Castle Lane in Belfast was a Catholic-owned business. Two Catholics died in the bomb blast there on 4 March 1972. Both were young women, Janet Bereen and Anne Owens. Two other women lost their legs. They had been in town shopping for their weddings. Those weddings went ahead when the women came out of hospital, providing the papers with strong images. The shock of this bomb was so great that a journalist feeding into a BBC news programme from the scene broke down and wept. We were in the office that night, speculating on who might have bombed the Abercorn. The victims were Catholics: it was a Catholic-owned restaurant but, in the media imagination, bombs were primarily an IRA weapon still, despite McGurk's bar. Therefore it must have been the IRA who had done it.

It was.

*The Sunday News* of the next morning made no attribution, however.

> Last night the RUC set up a disaster centre in police headquarters to deal with calls about the explosion. And patrol cars were touring the city trying to contact relatives of

> people injured in the blast. About 7 pounds of explosives were in the bomb which was planted in the crowded Catholic owned restaurant — a favourite haunt for young mothers and their families in town for an afternoon's shopping.

The report in the paper has the intimacy of an authentic eyewitness account, though the reporters aren't named. 'Doctors, nurses and first-aid workers moved among dozens of bodies laid out on the street, treating the injured for cuts, bruises and shock. As some of the injured staggered around dazed and others ran screaming hysterically in search of relatives, two inert bodies covered with blankers [*sic*] were carried by ambulance men from the wreckage.'

According to the report, injured people had run away without waiting for help.

> Out of the dust and smoke which belched from the wrecked building [a woman] saw a mother grasping her child in her arms and running blindly away from the devastation. Both were covered in blood and their clothes were ripped to shreds. And dozens of other people suffered a similar fate as they were slashed by slivers of glass which tore into the crowds outside. One teenage girl was seen walking away from the area apparently oblivious to the fact that blood was streaming from wounds in her head and face. Her leather coat was cut to tatters.

In a statement to the paper, Brian Faulkner recognised the bomb as the work of the IRA.

> What thought went through the twisted mind of the man who planted the bomb as, on the way out, he looked into the faces of the unsuspecting mothers and babies who were soon to be mutilated by the blast? Did he think of a United Ireland?
>
> If he did, then that aspiration is infinitely besmirched by this thought.

> Did he think he was drawing attention to the legal problems of internment and to the number of his captured IRA companions? If so, his very crime illustrates one of the major reasons why internment is necessary.

Was it easy sexism that overlooked the possibility that the Abercorn might have been bombed by women? The inquest would hear that two teenage girls were seen leaving a bag behind in the restaurant. A warning call came from a pub on the Falls Road two minutes before the explosion, making no mention of the Abercorn but just saying that there was a bomb in Castle Lane timed to go off in five minutes. What was the point of a useless warning? Was it a genuine but incompetent attempt to have the area cleared, or was it just a cosmetic endeavour that would allow the bombers to argue afterwards that it had not been their intention to kill civilians?

An unnamed surgeon issued a statement from the Royal Victoria Hospital: 'You are destroying not only the lives and hopes of individuals but the very joy of living in the country you profess to love. Just part of the casualty list tonight should be enough to make you realise how much you have destroyed which can never be restored. A male casualty, two legs amputated, female two legs one arm, female one leg one arm, female two legs.'

I danced, drunk, at a party with one of those women 15 years later. She fell over but laughed.

The week after the bomb, the IRA called a three-day ceasefire. *The Sunday News* pointed to four mediators between the Provisional IRA and the British government. The group of mediators did not include others whose names have been disclosed since, so traffic between the IRA leadership and Whitehall appears to have been busy.

After Bloody Sunday, the Derry priest Fr Denis Bradley established a link between the British and the IRA, with the help of a senior RUC officer, Frank Lagan. Their contact in the Northern Ireland Office was Frank Steele, but Steele had enough other connections to the IRA not to need to activate Bradley's team fully for another year. None of us knew anything about this at the time. Years later, Denis Bradley and I would become close friends and I would often stay with him and his family when I visited Derry. Denis is a rare type of man. He has a huge ego, combined with implacable discretion. I don't think I had ever seen that in anyone before. When I was in a tempestuous relationship in the late 1980s, it was Denis I visited for advice and consolation. I didn't know that, at the same time, he was also counselling Martin McGuinness on how to bring the IRA campaign to a close.

The IRA confirmed, in March 1972, just six weeks after Bloody Sunday, that talks with the British were under way. This was the first Provisional IRA ceasefire and the protocols of later years had not yet been established; and even during the ceasefire, the British army continued to pursue IRA men on the run and to make arrests. Westminster was blustering: 'We do not talk to murderers.' The IRA threatened to name the emissaries to prove that this was a lie.

Much of the press speculation about the three-day ceasefire suggested that the Provos simply needed a rest because they had lost so many operatives. A more likely theory, now, must be that British negotiators had demanded a ceasefire to establish that the IRA leadership was in full control of the organisation. The British were apparently anxious to agree an IRA response to their planned introduction of direct rule and the phasing out of internment. If that is correct, then William Craig, the Vanguard leader, was wrong to dismiss the ceasefire as a gimmick, as he did. It was a clear indication that the British were planning changes to the constitution of Northern Ireland, of the very kind that he had pledged to resist. A week later, Craig addressed a huge rally in the Ormeau Park in Belfast, at which he urged 70,000 people to get to know who the enemies of Ulster were.

'If the politicians fail, it will be our job to liquidate the enemy,' he declared. There was little room left for questioning whether Craig was promoting violent insurrection or not. 'Vanguard must have financial support for a fighting fund, not a publicity campaign but a fighting fund. We are going to do more than just talk.'

The rally opened with an announcement to shame the Unionist Party. All Stormont and Westminster MPs had been invited to join the rally. Only one had taken his place on the platform. That was the Westminster MP Mr James Molyneaux. The Rev. Martin Smith, not yet an MP, perhaps hadn't developed his political thinking to the point where he could recognise political motivation in others. He blamed the violence on papal negligence: 'We would have peace in our time if the Bishop of Rome would put his house in order.' And Billy Hull, president of the Loyalist Association of Workers, called for a mass mobilisation to crush terrorism. 'We cannot allow this murdering to carry on night after night. If the government does not mobilise the people, then we will have to mobilise ourselves.'

Many in the audience must have understood that Vanguard was asking them to identify republicans and wait for an order to kill them. Even so, it's an order that Craig never gave.

'It's about time you started giving us publicity,' said a man who imposed himself on our reporter when he was interviewing members of a Tartan gang. 'You write this: Derry [Bloody Sunday] was a picnic. Tell them that!'

Three weeks after the bombing of the Abercorn, on a bright spring day, I was walking through Andersonstown when a woman called me from her door. 'How are you, Malachi?'

'Grand now. How's it going?'

'Well, did you hear the news? We got two of the bastards in Donegall Street. That will cheer you up.'

I checked the news and heard that a car bomb had gone off

there and killed eight people. This was days before Faulkner was to meet Heath and was perhaps intended as a shocker to tip the discussions in favour of a Westminster takeover. That's not how the IRA members I have spoken to since recall it. They say that the job of phoning through the warning was delegated in advance to someone who was not on the bomb team and that the bomb team did not reach the intended target. Had they done so, the warning would have worked.

Another option might have been for the IRA to allow its teams to disarm bombs that could not be delivered on time. It didn't, so many civilians and IRA members died.

But political advantage flowed from this atrocity. If Heath, meeting Faulkner, had had any doubts about relieving him of responsibility for security in Northern Ireland, the high death toll in this one incident might have been expected to confirm his resolve. It made good tactical sense for this bomb to be bloody and shocking.

Tommy Gorman says: 'I felt deeply that we were achieving nothing by killing civilians; it didn't work.' On this occasion, perhaps it did. The bomb exploded farther down the street from our office but caused us no damage, though a story went round the building, a week later, that body parts had been found on the roof. There was a new strain in the atmosphere. Many of the journalists in the building had gone out to cover the explosion. Some took graphic photographs. Jim was disgusted by the *News Letter*'s coverage and its praise of the army's conduct.

'"Stark professionalism"! What the fuck is that?'

Earlier he had said to me, 'Don't walk about the building on your own.'

Some of the men from the print works below had been so enraged by the bomb that they had come to our office to see us about it. Who knows what they had in mind? 'It's all right. They have been spoken to. But it is as well this happened on a Monday' — when Jim and I were off.

That weekend I went on a press trip to Scotland. This was one of the standard junkets that journalists got. The Scottish Transport Ship Management Company had invited selected journalists to sample a new weekend break they were promoting. They were hoping to capitalise on the likelihood that people living in troubled Northern Ireland would want to get away as often as they could. This was what I needed. I went with eight other journalists from Northern Ireland, many of them from the provincial papers that we plundered for stories every week. There were the editors of the two Derry papers, the *Derry Journal* and the *Londonderry Sentinel.* These papers even accorded different names to the city they served, but the editors were friends.

I think I drank more whisky than water in the coming days. We were taken to restaurants and fed steaks that covered the whole plate. I had never in my life eaten so lavishly. As the youngest on the trip, I was adopted affectionately by the others. I told a joke that went down so well that I had to repeat it for every new person who joined the group, though the laughter paled on repetition. I think it was Colin, the sports editor, whom I'd first heard tell this one.

> A wee lad on the Falls Road is tearing round the corner when he bumps into a priest and knocks him over.
>
> The kid gets up and snarls at the priest. He says: 'Fuck you!'
>
> The priest is appalled, gets slowly to his feet, dusting himself down, and addresses the boy sternly: 'Have you no idea who I am, that you talk to me like that? Do you not know that I am a priest of Mother Church, responsible for the welfare of souls, imparting the grace of God? Do you not realise that as a priest here I could one day be your parish priest and that if I became parish priest, I could well go on to be the Bishop of this entire diocese.
>
> 'I will have you know that as Bishop I could actually be elevated to the holy College of Cardinals. Sonny, if I become a Cardinal I could be elected to the papacy. The papacy! I

could become Pope. Do you understand that?
Do you?
Fuck me, son? Fuck you!'

The night we left Belfast, Ted Heath, announced that he was going to prorogue the Stormont parliament. Faulkner was sacked. Though we were a bunch of professional journalists, this development would play only an incidental part in our weekend deliberations. As a mixed group, we would observe the niceties that said you shouldn't embarrass people on the other side by raising politics or religion with them. At a press conference, a tour operator described Loch Lomond as the largest stretch of inland waterway in the UK. A *News Letter* reporter corrected him: 'I think you'll find that that is Lough Neagh.' And there was much nervous laughter, with the Scots not being confident that they hadn't grossly insulted a sensitive guest.

We partied that night in Balloch, till five in the morning. I had the sense of having drunk myself sober again. When we arrived at the Dunblane Hydra, we were received with a tray of whiskies. At the disco, one of the tour guides was anxiously rubbing the imprint of his wedding ring from his finger. 'Some of the bitches would make a thing of it.'

I tried to get off with Isla, the go-go dancer, and promised to write to her. I couldn't coax her back to my room, though. The next day, we were to be driven to Callendar to see where *Dr Finlay's Casebook* had been filmed, when we heard that Vanguard was calling a general strike to protest against the closing of parliament. We raced through the Southern Uplands to get the last boat back from Stranraer to Larne before the strike started.

And suddenly it was as if Northern Ireland had a new flag, and it was everywhere. The Ulster flag, with the red cross on a white background and the red hand of Ulster at the centre, became the flag of protest against direct rule.

# Chapter 17

By the end of March 1972, three months into the year in which our paper had predicted the end of the violence and even agonised over how to retain its high circulation and hold the public interest when the violence had stopped, 96 people had died by bomb or bullet, 61 of them killed by one or other of the two wings of the IRA, mostly by the Provisionals. Ten of those IRA deaths had been own goals, that is, deaths caused by accidental explosions. Nineteen of the dead had been killed by the British army, and three — possibly five — by loyalists. Not every murder could be properly accounted for, but one thing was clear: the most violent year of the troubles so far had finished its first quarter and the killing rate was accelerating.

Brian Faulkner stood on the balcony at Stormont and said that Ulster would not be treated like a coconut colony, but the leadership of the protest fell to William Craig. On the front page of the 26 March edition, the paper carried a report of a call, from the Irish Congress of Trade Unions, for workers not to participate in the strike. Vanguard wanted all workers to strike on the Monday and Tuesday, 27 and 28 March. Craig emphasised that he wanted the police to join in the strike too. Coming from a former Minister of Home Affairs, who would have worked for years with the highest officers of the RUC, this was perhaps a key test of how credible and dangerous the threat from Craig was.

In fact, the Police Association rejected the idea. It said the RUC was 'a disciplined and impartial body dedicated to preserve [*sic*] the peace for the people of Northern Ireland. Appeals from other organisations for any formal strike or other action should be disregarded by our members.'

The strike call was also rejected by the Rev. Ian Paisley as 'utterly idiotic'. So unionism was split.

'Its only result will be to inflict wounds upon ourselves to no purpose. Do we want to destroy our own country?' Paisley said.

Craig's ambitions went beyond mere protest. The paper reported that he intended to form a provisional government to make direct rule unworkable. He repeated his threat to 'liquidate' the IRA, saying, 'We have the names, photographs and descriptions of more than 500 IRA men.' Craig also said that liquidation, in this case, would not entail shooting people, but he didn't clarify what he did mean by the word.

The paper reported that the Provisional IRA was divided on how to respond to direct rule. 'Speculation was growing' — though whose speculation isn't clear; perhaps just the reporter's — that Northern Provisionals were defying a 'fight on' order from the GCHQ in Dublin.

The SDLP, as the political party which represented most Catholics and which had been boycotting political talks and the Stormont parliament in protest against internment, was now claiming credit for bringing Stormont down. It was urging the IRA to end its campaign, as the surest way of ending internment and scrapping the Special Powers Act, under which it had been introduced. At a press conference in Belfast, John Hume addressed 'Protestant fellow citizens':

> We do not regard our political achievements as a victory over you, rather do we regard them as a step forward and as an opportunity for us all. We ask you to join us as equals on the road to permanent peace and justice and to add your considerable talents to ours so that we can build together in agreement a new society in which the sectarianism that has scourged our country will be an unhappy memory.

So, the naïveté in society, about the scale of the crisis, infected the SDLP too. It is inconceivable that the John Hume who wrote this statement had any idea that he would still be appealing to Northern Protestants, in similar language, 30 years later, to recognise his party as an ally. But Hume clearly knew that Stormont, in its old form, was not coming back and that the government would end internment to meet his conditions for entering negotiations on a new form of government.

The paper reported that two members of the SDLP, Ivan Cooper and Paddy Devlin, had travelled to Dublin, to appeal to the IRA leader Seán MacStíofáin to reconsider his decision not to call off the IRA campaign. Both the SDLP and the republican movement refused to confirm or deny that they had met — a sure sign that they had.

The Alliance Party, meeting that weekend, showed little grasp of British government intentions. The party's parliamentary leader, Phelim O'Neill, described the introduction of direct rule as 'purely a move to find a new way of restoring the rule of law'. He said: 'I am perfectly certain that Mr Heath will be anxious to restore the original parliament as soon as possible and I am entirely in favour of this.'

But this was more than a security initiative; it was the start of a serious attempt at political reform and the end of the majority rule which, in a divided society, allowed one community to legislate for the other.

The Stormont parliament's last exercise of executive power, before being shut down by London, was a measure to secure the towns and cities of Northern Ireland against car bombs. It gave the police and local authorities the right to impose extensive parking restrictions. Had the IRA accepted a trade-off of direct rule and the release of internees for an end to its campaign, the new law would not have been needed. In fact, it reshaped urban life for the next 22 years.

There was a new anger in Belfast, and loyalists built barricades to match the more permanent republican ones. That Saturday night, the taxi taking me home detoured into the Shankill Road and into streets governed by loyalists in black masks.

'Are you wise?' I said to the driver.

On a previous Saturday, when we had been stopped at an IRA roadblock, I had got out and asked the IRA man to show me his gun, an Armalite. Perhaps this was the taxi company's revenge. 'Sure I'm up and down here every day.'

If there was going to be the 'Protestant backlash' we'd all been waiting for, surely now was the time for it.

Journalism was an intrusive job. We usually cared more about the story we would write than about those we interviewed. Sometimes the people protested that we had treated them shoddily. I wrote a story about alcoholics drinking in doorways around Chapel Lane. I went with a photographer to try to interview one gruff man in a tweed overcoat, who was drinking a half bottle of South African wine on a doorstep. I coaxed him into posing for a photograph. On the following Tuesday morning, when I arrived at work, he was in reception, roaring his hurt outrage at the demure young receptionist. He recognised me and started waving the paper at me, with his appalling picture in it. I wasn't sure what his objection was. Did he not know what he looked like, what his life had become? But his anger was plain until I gave him 50p and he went away quietly. The girl at reception had no pity for him. 'I would have given him nothing,' she said.

I thought he had let me off lightly and wished I had given him more.

One Saturday night, Jim asked Stephen and me to go to the Oldpark area to report on the killing of an eight-year-old girl, Rosaleen Gavin. I assumed that, at best, someone might speak to us on the doorstep. What right had we to intrude? Maybe a neighbour would help us out with things like the name of the school the dead girl went to, or if she had brothers and sisters. I've never felt as helpless as a journalist. The woman who answered the door brought us in. I wasn't ready for that. The Gavins were confused and distraught and, strangely, our arrival gave them something to focus on. They made us sit down and have a cup of tea.

The visit to the home of Rosaleen Gavin was one of my first experiences in adult life of a death house. I had been around my friend Fegan when his father died a year earlier, but at more of a distance.

The women in the Gavin family were immediately concerned for our welfare and comfort, but that is how people usually do behave in a death house. They become attentive to the visitor. That is their alternative to dwelling constantly on their loss. 'You poor boy,' one said to me — to a reporter, an intruder. They made me sit in an armchair. A woman got out of it to make room for me.

'Did you get a picture of the girl?' asked Jim. 'I did one of those jobs once and I had my arm over the shoulder of the woman consoling her and reaching at the same time for a wee picture on the table beside her. That's what you have to do.'

It wasn't like that at all. We couldn't care any more about the story or the deadline. We just sat there and absorbed the shock and the horror. Rosaleen's mother sat beside me, almost demented, and said: 'You poor boy, you poor boy.'

What can she have been thinking of?

Stephen must have written up the story or given the information to Jim. It was the front-page lead. Rosaleen had been killed by an IRA sniper. There was no burden this campaign would not impose on the people who lived there.

# Chapter 18

One Saturday, I went into Kelly's and a guy called Dessie, who is now a rich businessman, was sitting disconsolately on the bench at the back wall. 'What gives?'

'They have shot McCann.'

In those days of much discretion, people often assumed you knew more than you did. 'Which McCann?'

'Joe McCann.'

I had no idea who Joe McCann was.

'Sure you were drinking with him in Kelly's last week,' said Jim.

I couldn't place him.

'Do you know Ciaran Donnelly's picture of the guy with the M1 carbine, down at the Markets on internment day?'

Donnelly was one of the better young photographers. His picture of McCann has since been used on the cover of Henry McDonald's book *Colours*, and on a U2 album cover. It shows McCann crouching casually against a backdrop of flames, one hand holding his rifle. There is battlefield rubble on the street around him.

Joe McCann had been spotted that afternoon in Joy Street by a Special Branch officer, Harry Taylor. Soldiers who joined the chase shot him in the back as he ran.

'Harry Taylor used to drive me home from college,' I said.

'Don't tell that to anyone in Kelly's,' said Jim.

McCann's death was a big event in the life of the paper. Jim wrote a tribute to him the following week. In this, he was stretching the boundaries of the paper's ethos. Already there had been several stories that paid more respect to the republicans, and some of the loyalists too, than the culture of the building around us could happily absorb. We enjoyed flexing the unwritten rule. We rationalised that the intelligent reader could spot the anomalies anyway, like when we reported that republicans in Strabane wanted local traders to take down security hoardings because they were an 'eyesore'. Did publishing such a ridiculous story validate it or was it an act of irony? It was for the reader to decide.

The article on Joe McCann was almost a eulogy. 'In the lower Falls, stories are still told of his deeds during the battle of the Falls in July 1970. It was the first stand-up fight against the troops in Ireland since 1916.'

This was complete nonsense. The 'stand-up fight' was nothing of the kind or somebody would have been killed. Four people did die during that period. They were all unarmed civilians killed by the army; one of them was run over by a military vehicle. No one was killed in exchanges of fire between the army and the IRA because the gunmen took better care not to be shot than the ordinary civilians on the street did, even though this prevented them from actually shooting anyone either.

Another occasion on which McCann was credited with noble heroics was during the first internment raids on 9 August 1971, the day Frank McGuinness was shot dead on our street corner beside Tommy Gorman. In the Markets area, when soldiers came to raid houses, 'McCann himself acted as a rearguard gunner, pinning down the advancing troops with a hail of fire.'

When the article described McCann as the 'Che Guevara of the IRA' it meant perhaps that he had the potential to become a popular myth, a myth that the paper was amenable to helping. It could hardly have meant that he had had as busy a career as a revolutionary fighter.

McCann, said the article, had joined the IRA in the early 1960s as the '56–'62 campaign was fizzling out. He would have been about 15 then. In 1966, at the age of 18 or 19, he was arrested outside an army base, wearing a khaki battle tunic and with a bayonet concealed in his car. He served six months in jail for that. He had been active in political campaigns, like the Belfast Housing Action Group — in which presumably he too had opposed the building of the ring road on the grounds that it would divide Protestant and Catholic — and a campaign against Irish membership of the Common Market.

You can't help but form the impression sometimes, reading these stories, that people like McCann, and those who admired him, had little realistic grasp of the pain they were bringing upon those they claimed to represent.

Though I had not known Joe McCann well enough to recall his face after he had been shot, I did get to know some of the other Stickies from his patch — the Markets. (The Official IRA were called the Stickies because, at the Easter commemoration in 1970, after the Provisionals had split from them, they issued different Easter Lily badges: the Provisionals issued paper badges with a pin for the lapel, and the Officials issued badges with adhesive — sticky — backs. The hostility between these groups ran deep and had already erupted in shooting feuds and deaths.)

I first met Tommy Conlon when Jim asked me to go into the Markets to do a story about how the Stickies had squatted in a vacant tannery and converted it into a drinking club. It was a simple story, one of the stories that might be told in a tone of wounded disapproval in another paper but which ran with a little levity in ours. Tony Rosatto was with Tommy when I met him. I had known Tony before and often drank with his brothers, Kevin and Martin, in Kelly's Cellars.

Later, Councillor Paddy Wilson of the SDLP came to me with a story about plans to close some educational facility in the Markets area. 'It's not much of a story,' said Paddy, a big, round-headed, balding man. 'Do what you like with it.' What I did enraged him. I went to Tommy and got a quote from the Stickies, thinking that was a clever thing to do. Paddy, who had seemed uninterested at first, now felt the loss of an opportunity to promote his own party's social concern.

'We got nothing out of that,' he said, scowling at me. 'Nothing.'

A simple lesson learned the hard way: any politician who gives you any story will resent a rival getting credit for it. The irony is that it had been so hard to get a quote from the Stickies in the first place. 'Look, we have a fucking war on. Go and ask somebody else,' said one of them.

I began going socially to the Stickie drinking den in the Markets with Maguire and Fegan. Already Joe McCann had had songs written about him. A blonde woman took the stage for the most solemn moment every Sunday night: 'They have murdered our hero, brave Jo-seph McCaaaaaann.'

By this stage, Jim's friend Chris, who had brought the beer barrel to the office for Christmas, had left the brewery and was working as a freelance journalist. He had made an arrangement with the *Sunday Independent*. Jim took me aside one day and asked me to be as helpful as I could. One Saturday, a story had gone out about a plan by the Official IRA to fire mortars over the Belfast peace line, into Protestant areas. Jim suggested that I take Chris to meet the Stickies and ask if there was any truth in it.

'Let's go to the Markets,' I said.

'No,' said Chris. 'Let's go and see Kitty up in Leeson Street.'

The taxi pulled up outside The Long Bar and Chris stuck

his press card out the window to show a group of lads. '*Sunday Independent.* Is Kitty about?'

I didn't like being so conspicuous but, in fairness to Chris, it might have been a good defence. Nobody could quickly shuffle you round a corner and up an alley if everybody was looking at you. Chris later got a name for being one of the boldest journalists in dealings with loyalist paramilitaries; the very thought of going near them terrified me. Kitty came out and said: 'Let's go to the Markets and ask Conlon what he knows about this.'

Our story was that the Officials denied having issued the statement and had no intention of mortaring Protestants.

I felt it was unfair to me that war had surrounded me. I was 21. I had a good job with a salary, though I was spending it all. I should have been able to enjoy life without fear. I should have had a girlfriend and a car. But finding a girlfriend then seemed impossible. There was a girl called Geraldine who would meet me for walks but where could you walk to? Geraldine was determined to ignore the threat. One day, she said to me: 'When there's shooting, what's that sound like bees buzzing?'

I asked Jim. He laughed: 'It's the bullets whizzing past your head, stupid.'

Geraldine would not concede anything to the gunmen. Even to take cover from them dignified their purpose, as far as she was concerned. One night, we were walking past the back of the bus station. Ahead was Sandy Row, a loyalist area. I said: 'We can't go there; it isn't safe.' She walked on. All the street lights were out. There was anti-Catholic graffiti on the walls. No vigilantes stopped us. Perhaps the people there were frightened too and were staying off the street.

On a Sunday afternoon, we walked down Blacks Road at Dunmurry. Up ahead of us, we saw a dozen boys in bright-red tartan scarves — Protestant street fighters. If we didn't want to be kicked to death — and I didn't — we would have been better turning back into a clear Catholic area.

'We're not bothering them,' said Geraldine. And we walked on through them. They, of course, assumed that no sane Catholic would have dared approach them so they didn't consider that we could be Catholics.

Another night, we propped ourselves against the back wall of a shop. I was still, in my head, a teenager. I had the money to take her to a nice restaurant or a hotel but I had no habit or experience of leisure beyond drinking, or of intimacy beyond wrestling in the dark. Suddenly the night air was ripped by a long spurt from a submachine-gun. I was no judge of guns, though everybody then seemed to think they could identify them by their sound. But there was something very clear and clean about this burst, as if from a technically neater and cleaner weapon. Just one burst. Perhaps a dozen individual bullets. It killed the mood. That burst of gunfire had come from close to my home. Soldiers in a car had approached the Riverdale barricade and had shot Patsy McVeigh, an IRA auxiliary.

I met Geraldine again the next night and she said it was over. I had no idea why. Maybe she just realised I was a desperate, hungry man; maybe she was sick of gunfire; maybe I had B.O. That was life at the time: you couldn't tell the mundane from the horrific.

People were obsessed with news. I had a brief dalliance with Carmel, whose mother would be sitting up listening to the police radio at one o'clock in the morning, when we went back to her house. Carmel's mother detested the IRA: 'Do you know Eddie Carmichael?' Carmichael was one of the E Company lads. 'He's a stinking get,' she declared.

The trouble encroached too on ordinary friendships. Nights out drinking with Fegan and Maguire usually ended with me and Maguire sitting in his car outside my home in Riverdale, having the last fag of the night and hankering for a life that was more free and more sexual. Maguire was the first person I ever had thoughtful conversations with, usually lit by the glow of his fag in the car under a dead street light whose clock timer a bomb-maker — perhaps Tommy Gorman — had stolen. Conversation was the only joy there was space for. One night, a man tapped on the window of the car. Maguire wound it down. It wasn't a man but a boy of about 16, with curly hair.

'What's going on here, then?'

We both would have liked to tell him to fuck off but he had probably been sent by Tucker Kane and had to report back to him. 'I live here,' I said, trying to make it sound sarcastic. I was one of those he was supposedly protecting.

'My fear', said Maguire afterwards, 'is that some day one of those fuckers will put a gun in my hand and post me on a corner. It can't suit them that people living under their noses will have nothing to do with them. They're probably discussing right now how to deal with us.'

One day, a boy pulled a gun on Maguire as he was getting out of his car and demanded the keys. Maguire told him to fuck off and threw the keys into a garden. His calculation was that the boy would see no point in shooting him once the chance of getting the keys was lost. But not everyone would have been cool enough to make a calculation like that and stake his life on it.

# Chapter 19

Stormont was gone. Those who could read British intentions, like John Hume and probably Brian Faulkner, knew that it would not come back, that the only form of government Northern Ireland would ever get now would be one which nationalists helped to design. Craig knew that the loss of Stormont created new options, and he wanted to close them down, so he argued for the creation of a provisional government. Paisley knew that was a bad plan. But what of the IRA? It could choose to take the credit for having defeated Faulkner, brought down Stormont and cleared the way for nationalists to share power, or it could fight on for the removal of Britain from Ireland. It made a choice that was every bit as stupid as Craig's: it opted to fight for the unattainable.

*The Sunday News* reported that not all Provisionals agreed with this decision. On 2 April, it carried a story that Dutch Doherty, one of the escapers from Crumlin Road prison, had been expelled from the IRA, ostensibly for recognising a court in the Irish Republic. A republican ideologue at that time was expected to refuse the jurisdiction of all Irish courts, north and south, the IRA regarding itself as the only legitimate power on the island. The paper said that this was really about Northern IRA members wanting a one-month truce.

> The Provisional leadership in Dublin took a tough line over this truce and, after hurried consultation between [*sic*] the Northern leader who ordered it the truce order was rescinded.

The Provos were also under pressure from within the Catholic community. On Friday, 31 March, a mother of ten, Martha Crawford, had been killed during a gun battle in Rosnareen Avenue. Both the army and the IRA denied that it was one of their bullets which had struck her, but a delegation of local women pleaded with the IRA leadership to stop putting people in danger.

At a public meeting in the Brandywell in Derry, a Derry IRA leader, Martin McGuinness, rejected the SDLP's appeal for a truce. The paper described him as one of the most wanted of the Provisional IRA leaders and 'Officer commanding the local Provisional IRA brigade'. He has since said that he was second in command at that time. McGuinness and Daithí Ó Conaill — called David O'Connell by *The Sunday News* which preferred to use the English form of Irish names — announced that they would establish the machinery for local elections to prove that the SDLP was not legitimately representative of the people in the area.

Máire Drumm spoke at the meeting and attacked the disloyalty of those who wanted a ceasefire: 'If you insist on the truce some people are calling for, if you refuse to back up the boys who are fighting the British army, and if the British army comes in and murders you, I say "good luck to them" for you deserve to be murdered.'

It was an incredibly brash thing to say in the city that had suffered Bloody Sunday. I knew Máire. One of her sons had been in the same class as me in primary school. I had danced with one of her daughters at a teenage céilidh. They were gentle people. She was coarse and loud but laughed too. Her husband Jim was the one the children took their soft manners from, I think. Yet he was one of the founders of the Provisional IRA. Work that out. These were the Father and Mother of the bombing campaign. I wonder how Máire would have dealt with the two young women who bombed the Abercorn.

'We all make mistakes; put it behind you.'

Or:

'That'll show them the mess we are ready to make of this place if they don't give us what we want.'

In Derry, she had said that those who didn't back the IRA deserved to be murdered. That would have included many of those who had been killed on Bloody Sunday. It would have included many of those who were in the Abercorn when the IRA girls bombed it. It included me. My friend Fegan's mother was one of the women organising an appeal to the IRA to end the campaign. At the same time, the IRA was building more permanent barricades, using diggers and drills. Fegan's mother had a meeting with Séamus Twomey, the local commander. On a Sunday afternoon, I went to watch one of Máire Drumm's meetings for rallying support for the IRA. She was in scalding form, attacking Fegan's mother and the other traitors to the cause who would betray the IRA.

'That's what your ma is up against,' I said. It was clear she hadn't a chance. She could hardly be sure that Mrs Drumm wouldn't scratch her eyes out if she came near her. For Máire Drumm was one of those who had no doubt at all that the bombing campaign by the Provos was a legitimate and necessary war for the liberation of Ireland from the British. Any Irish person who could not see that, and who got squeamish about the killing, was simply contemptible in her eyes.

To me, she was a marvel, an oddity. For all that she scowled at half-hearted nationalists and republicans, it was she who was the rarity. I didn't know any other person with her strength of conviction. Or did that mean that it was I who was out of touch with the feelings of the people I lived among? I don't think so. For one thing, many others who agreed with Máire Drumm about the need to arm and defend the Catholics did it through other organisations and with different ideologies to support them.

The Official IRA was socialist and already planning to give up its armed campaign, ostensibly at least, because it was inflicting too much pain on the working classes. There was the Catholic Ex-Servicemen's Association. My friend Philip was in that. The group was set up by former soldiers at a time when you could expect to be held in high regard in west Belfast for having been a member of the British army. Philip and others kitted themselves out like a football team and took a coach south for rifle training. The CESA plan was simply to build and maintain a militia that would be on hand to defend Catholic neighbourhoods if they were attacked by Protestants again. They had no plan to fight for a united Ireland or to overthrow the capitalist system.

It was because there were these diverse assessments of how to represent Catholics, with and without arms, that Máire Drumm had to astonish us with her passion and dogma. She was barking at us because she was in danger of losing the argument that the IRA had to fight on.

Sensible people thought that the game was up now for the IRA. Eugene O'Hara, a Derry Catholic, addressed the United Nations Association in Reading. He said: 'I am certain that violence is now diminishing and please God, it will go on doing so.'

# Part Four

# Chapter 20

What I have learnt from looking back at the political and media climate of 1972 is that we were all naïve and immature in the face of crisis. The historian A.T.Q. Stewart has written about how violence returned to Belfast like the nineteenth century crashing up through the cobbles. Some people reacted immediately to what was familiar to them. They knew what to do because their parents and their grandparents had told them what they had done. But it wasn't so familiar to everyone.

While I once blamed myself for having been so immature and incompetent, I can see now that I was part of a hapless and bewildered generation. I have spoken to one of the men who led the UDA in that period. This is a man who would have had me killed had I strayed into his company back then. He said:

> I don't remember much about it. I don't think about it. It is too confusing. A lot of us live with regret and don't say so. We can't explain why we did what we did. We were being used: that's part of it. But the more you think of it, the more you

conclude that you were just vicious and stupid and you blame yourself — and that can't be the whole story.

However, if he has little sense now of why he led a huge organisation committed to protest and murder on behalf of loyalism, it is possible that many of those on the other side, who led the Provisional IRA, were equally motivated by ill-formed notions.

It is appalling how naïve people were. Bernadette Devlin, who inspired many radicals then, told *Playboy* magazine that she wanted the British to leave, knowing that this would create a civil war. We could then have a socialist republic and fund it by nationalising the mines, she said.

It is a little reassuring to see that even the *Playboy* of those days looks quaint and coy. This was a time when it had just become permissible to show pubic hair on models, but not the actual vagina, so hair had to be copious and bushy.

The IRA had grown in size rapidly from 1970. Most of its new members were young men and women in Belfast and Derry. They were inducted into republican militarism by older people like the Drumms, who had the tradition in their blood. Had that generation not survived, and had they not still had their intact structures, who knows where the fear and anger of young men in Northern Ireland would have been directed in the 1970s?

We were different from the rest of Europe before 1972 because we had had no experience of war in our generation. The rest of Europe had been soaked in blood less than three decades earlier. We had not been part of that. Had that woman, who called out to me to share the good news of a bombing in town, grown up in England, she might have had a father who had gone away, maybe come back with a foot blown off or an eye out — if he had come back at all — and the first time he had heard her say, as a child or teenager, that war was a good thing, he would have corrected her, perhaps bluntly.

For all our romanticism about 1916 and the IRA campaigns, these were small flirtations with war, not comparable to the experience of England or Germany. But give us another 20 years of this and there would be no lust for it left. Ironically, by then, England and America would be ripe for a fresh taste of it.

In 1972, Northern Ireland was divided on whether or not to fight a war. That debate ran through the Provisionals themselves, with some recommending a truce. It divided loyalism too. The loyalist gangs would have their own revenge on Catholics by killing them, singly and at random. Could it have gone the other way? The Official IRA swung against war. The Catholic Ex-Servicemen's Association armed itself for defence only. But there was no vote on it; it was not a collective decision. Those who wanted war would have it, regardless of what others wanted. Máire Drumm's excoriation amounted to a denial to the rest of us of any say in the matter.

'You deserve to be murdered,' she had said.

The new Secretary of State, William Whitelaw, had the measure of the problem when he said, in April 1972, that there were people in Northern Ireland so consumed with bitterness that they did not want him to succeed in bringing peace. 'They will try to panic me from leading in the cause of peaceful persuasion: they will try to tempt me into escalating military repression, which will solve nothing and only increase bitter strife within the community.'

He was right in saying that the paramilitaries would try to tempt him into a military crackdown. He was wrong in his confidence that they would fail. The problem was that people were being driven to violence by more than irrational bitterness; they were still confident, some of them, that violence would deliver the political results they sought. That experiment had yet to fail comprehensively.

The ghastly lives that many people were living is clear in a report I did for *The Sunday News* about Divis Flats. The Housing Executive was looking for a new caretaker because Thomas Mullaney could take no more. 'They start shooting in the afternoon and carry on right through the night. In the mornings they sleep it off for a few hours and wake up ready to start again.'

Mr Mullaney told me: 'Last week, gunmen asked me to turn out the lights on the balconies and I refused. They said that if I didn't they would smash them, so I had to.'

If you were to evaluate the conduct of many in the Provisional IRA on pragmatic grounds, or in terms of ordinary criminal common sense, it was reckless. Those men should not have been so public in their activities. That endangered them as well as imposing the burden of knowledge on those who did not support them. The IRA men could have secured themselves better and imposed less secrecy on those who weren't up to it, simply by hiding their guns properly. But no, they bullied the caretaker at Divis Flats into turning the lights out for them. And later in the year, at the same flats, they kidnapped and murdered Jean McConville, a mother of seven children, because they thought she was telling others what they were doing. Why, a proper conspirator would ask, did they have to let Jean McConville know what they were doing in the first place? It was a question raised by Fr Denis Bradley, after the Provos shot a teenage boy for informing. From the pulpit, he sneered at them: if he knew, how did he know? — only because you lot hadn't the sense to be more discreet.

With the incessant violence, all civic development in some areas ground to a halt. Alliance Party councillor Tom Sherry protested that work in Andersonstown to build a swimming pool, a health centre, football pitches and houses had all stopped because contractors could not get insurance companies to indemnify them. Sherry said:

> In the past we have had assurances from the IRA that equipment would not be damaged and a guard would be placed upon it to ensure that vandals in the area caused no damage. But tell that to an insurance company. The only guarantee that they will listen to it is a period of peace.

So, though the Provisional IRA was an illegal revolutionary organisation, intent on murder and destruction on a massive scale, even as early as 1972 it was acquiring a recognised role within the institutions of the state; local government representatives had asked it to provide safe passage for workers and protection for building projects, and presumably trusted its undertakings.

Guns and gunmen were integral to our lives, public and domestic. One day a boy called 'Ardo' knocked on our back door and asked if he could come in and fix his jammed rifle. He knelt over it on the living-room floor and wrestled with the bolt until he had cleared a bullet.

'Och, thanks, Mrs O'Doherty,' he said. 'Jimmy would kill me if he knew.'

# Chapter 21

Loyalists were stepping up their own armed campaign. On 13 May, they wrecked Kelly's Tavern in Ballymurphy with a car bomb and opened fire on the fleeing survivors. This was a huge front-page story for the paper on the following day. Republicans exchanged hundreds of shots with loyalist snipers and also attacked the British army, killing one soldier and wounding one in the face, according to our report. The final toll was higher, with five dead there.

> Sixty people were rushed to hospital in a fleet of ambulances. As civilians gathered at the scene to help in the rescue operation, several shots rang out, forcing them to dive for cover.

Eddie and Stephen covered that story. Stephen recalls both of them taking cover as the army fired from a large gun over their heads into the City Cemetery.

There was another detailed story from the same area. An IRA gang had tried to rob the Springfield Road branch of the Co-op supermarket. The deputy manager, Paddy O'Loughlin, refused to open the till for them. 'I wasn't giving them anything but one of the girls got frightened and thought they might shoot me so she flicked the catch and let them at the money.'

Plainclothes detectives came into the shop and overpowered the robbers.

One of the decisive features of the later troubles was prison protest, but this was new to us in 1972 and we had little sense of how crucial it would be to the political strategy of the IRA, and how successful it would ultimately be in rallying popular support around the movement. On 7 May, *The Sunday News* reported that republican and loyalist prisoners were to co-operate in a campaign for political status. A week later, the paper reported that the loyalists were yet to join the protests. This was to be a big campaign for the Provisionals and they would succeed in it.

The coverage of an IRA hunger strike was low-key in *The Sunday News*, but the hunger strike proved to be a greater driving force for change than the loyalist barricades or even the bombing campaign. The prisoners, of both the Provisional and Official IRA, were, according to the paper, claiming political status for themselves and for the loyalists. *The Sunday News* was keen to write the loyalists into the story of the protest but there appears to have been little basis for this, other than the hopes of some of the Officials to cross the divide and represent broad working-class interests.

The success of the prison campaign would resonate for decades. The first lesson learnt would be that hunger-striking works. The prisoners in 1972 won Special Category Status. The withdrawal of that status would trigger two mass hunger strikes in 1980 and 1981, and the effective restoration of it after 1981 would condition the character of the Agreement in 1998. We wrote about the 1972 hunger strike without the retrospective understanding of its huge political impact, but the story included one astute prediction:

> And in the long-term, political prisoner status would also mean that republicans and loyalists — either jointly or separately — could press the Westminster administration in Ulster in negotiating an amnesty.

What seemed then to be the most fanciful part of that prediction is the suggestion that loyalists or republicans would work jointly for an amnesty — but they would. What they achieved in 1998, though, was not a full amnesty but early mass releases for those paramilitaries who backed political parties which supported the Agreement. By that point, any suggestion that they were not really political prisoners would be a semantic quibble.

A more quaint idea in the paper's discussion of the hunger strike was a suggestion that prisoners might fight through the civil courts to defend their dignity against government propaganda. One group of Official IRA hunger strikers emphatically denied government suggestions that they were secretly eating. They were so outraged that they threatened to sue the Ministry of Home Affairs for defamation of character. It sank in with paramilitaries later on that criminal convictions for acts of murder stripped people of any character that a jury would be inclined to defend.

In many other ways, this protest and its management on both sides anticipated the conduct of the peace process of the 1990s. We would later be familiar with the tactic of politicians using public speeches to communicate their positions and even answer questions from the IRA.

At a time when the IRA was testing the British to see how much they might concede constitutionally, Edward Heath made a speech to the Scottish Conservative Party which his mediators will have urged the IRA to read. Heath ruled out both total British withdrawal from Northern Ireland and a military solution. He was determined to seek conciliation, he said. And when he introduced direct rule, he was 'affirming that the status of Northern Ireland as part of the UK would not be changed except by consent.'

The IRA might have read some flexibility into this but only in relation to how Northern Ireland might be governed within the UK. Heath was also trying to assure the loyalists that he understood their concerns.

> I suppose there is no one more proud of their historic place in the UK than the Protestant majority in Northern Ireland. Where one nation means one British nation within the UK, they would be foremost in its defence. But they must know you cannot create one nation unless it is balanced.

There was a flaw in Heath's policy; he wanted political compromise rather than military victory, but success would depend on the IRA's being willing to end its campaign on a settlement short of a united Ireland. Without that, he would be compelled to try to defeat the organisation. And failing that, where would he be?

He would be pushed by the IRA into that paradoxical position before the summer was out.

In the early hours of 2 May, a bomb in Belfast's Short Strand forced a total rewrite of our front page: 'Four Killed in Bomb Horror'. The bomb blast completely flattened two family homes. In fact, eight people were killed, and four of them were IRA members.

'The car bomb, which was spotted by a group of youths before it exploded, wrecked half of Anderson Street,' said the paper. 'It's like the Blitz, only worse. Several of our neighbours are dead,' one woman told a reporter.

The bomb, which is now acknowledged to have been one of the IRA's own, produced the biggest loss of life in Short Strand of any incident of the troubles. It was an embarrassment to the IRA because Short Strand, surrounded by Protestant areas, was central to the IRA myth that its members were the defenders of the Catholic people. The bomb had exploded in transit. The IRA admitted this in *Tírghrá*, a tribute to the organisation's dead, published in 2002. Our reporter can hardly have been expected to get right to the heart of such a story, and the achievement of putting together a detailed report from the scene was considerable, perhaps the finest job done by a reporter on that paper at that time. Our 5 a.m. update on that story, confirming four dead and 13 injured, quoted a police statement: 'In some cases all we have are remnants of bodies in plastic bags.'

The following week, the paper led with a report on the loyalist barricades. The UDA was sealing off scores of streets throughout the city, in protest against government toleration of no-go areas controlled by the IRA. But the paper assumed that a substantial part of its readership was still more interested in glib sexual generalisations than in the collapse of order in the capital. Hilariously beside the main lead was a blurb for an inside story, 'in praise of older men'.

> Read what wives and mistresses have to say about their older lovers: men over 40 and under 60 are the only good lovers. They alone know how to handle a woman.

It's a wonder that anyone had emotional energy to spare for love, with the city in such a state. 'By late evening, a few main roads leading from Belfast were open to traffic,' reported the paper. 'Throughout the day, members of the Ulster Defence Association drilled in military fashion behind barricades with security patrols watching on.'

How, the paper might have asked, could any woman keep an assignation with her older man on a night like that, assuming for a start that he had the sense not to be parading behind a barricade himself?

Enoch Powell visited Northern Ireland that week and

shared a platform with rivals William Craig, the Vanguard leader, and Brian Faulkner, the deposed Prime Minister. The meeting was presented by the headline writer as a demonstration of loyalist unity. Unity was what Faulkner and Powell wanted, but Craig was still predicting a revolt. He was calling on loyalists to get together to write their own constitution, in defiance of the government. Over the next two or three weeks, he said, the whole world would see that the British government now governed Ulster without the consent of the people. If this was an ominous sign of growing disorder, another was the report that the Provisional IRA was importing Japanese AR 180s, collapsible Armalites, rifles more effective than the SLRs used by the British army itself.

The rapid growth of the paramilitary groups also provided business for army surplus stores in Belfast's Smithfield market and we reported that loyalists and republicans were both buying their jackets, hats and boots from the same shops. The type of jacket favoured by the UDA was selling then for £2.50. The shops were not selling much to Vanguard, which still drilled in civilian clothes, though a picture of Major F.R.A. Hynds, inspecting the Belfast Orange Volunteers alongside William Craig, showed Hynds and a companion sporting their war medals. Hynds had earned his medals on D-day. The commendation for his Military Cross read:

> Major Hynds showed great gallantry and outstanding courage when he purposely exposed himself to small arms fire and concentrated artillery fire in order to encourage and steady his men and assist in the evacuation of the wounded.

However, he was 79 years old now and perhaps more warmly appreciated for being an Orangeman, a former deputy Grand Master, than for any readiness to steady the nerves of the men of Ulster Vanguard by exposing himself to the rifles of the

IRA. The officers commanding this group wore maroon berets. Vanguard and the Orange Volunteers did not erect barricades but, the paper reported, Belfast city centre was closed to traffic for several hours to make way for them, so they were just as disruptive.

'Brighten Your Days With Ulster's Leading Sunday Newspaper,' said a strap line across the top of the front page on 18 June.

'Bombers Hit at Pubs,' said the headline below it.

That issue reported speculation that IRA Chief of Staff Seán MacStíofáin had been ousted. This was two days before the Secretary of State's emissary, P.J. Woodfield, had a secret meeting with IRA leaders Gerry Adams and Daithí Ó Conaill in County Donegal. Even by the *Sunday News* style of speculative reportage, this was a thin story. Certainly, Mr Woodfield, speaking to Adams and Ó Conaill, didn't seem to give any credence to it.

## Chapter 22

The first major result of the political machinations to coax the IRA into a ceasefire was a declaration from the Official IRA, which called a ceasefire in June 1972. The ostensible reason for this was that outrage, over the Officials' murder of a young Catholic soldier in Derry, had proven hard to bear. But can it have been to their political advantage to be seen to be reacting to emotional pressure when they had good reasons anyway for calling off the campaign? They could have claimed a victory after the introduction of direct rule but it was too late for that now; that would have been an admission that the killing since had indeed been pointless murder. Perhaps they thought that ending the campaign, ostensibly in response to community pressure, would make them seem more considerate of the needs of the people than the Provisionals were. That wouldn't have been hard, though.

But how must they have felt two weeks later to see that the Provisionals had called a ceasefire and gone straight into negotiations with the Secretary of State and the British government? Did they feel they had lost an opportunity? Only if they believed the Provisionals were going into talks with a realistic expectation of advancing their cause, and they weren't. Clearly, though, the Official ceasefire made the Provisionals' intimation of willingness to end their campaign more plausible. The British would have seen little point in making a truce with the Provos alone if the Officials had still been killing soldiers in Belfast and Derry. The Provisonals would have been put in the embarrassing position of having to disown every killing of a soldier by the Officials, and Officials still at war would have been in a position to accuse the Provisionals of selling out the cause for political advantage. Whatever the thinking, the Provisional ceasefire would have been impossible without a ceasefire by the Officials preceding it. It came two weeks after it.

Stephen said that he would love to get a picture for the wire services of a young Provo hanging up his gun. 'Surely it would do no harm to ask.' On the afternoon that the Provisional IRA announced it would order a ceasefire, I walked down the middle of Royal Avenue, waving my arms in the rain like a drunken man. This was fantastic news. 'But all you have to do is ask one of them. Imagine the picture; he is hanging up his gun, putting it away — his war is over.'

One of those I could have asked was Tommy Gorman, if I had been on speaking terms with him then. Tommy's E Company attended a battalion briefing from Seán MacStíofáin, the IRA Chief of Staff. He told them not to expect the ceasefire to last long or to produce a political result. The IRA made sure that the shooting did not stop until the dot of midnight on Sunday, the date when they said the ceasefire would start. Two of our local Provos were arrested, trying out a robbery on the last day.

'Do you really believe it is over now?' asked Stephen.

I didn't know. I wanted it to be over.

The atmosphere in Belfast changed immediately. The British soldiers slung their rifles over their shoulders and wore berets instead of helmets, to signal their trust in the IRA. Where they had continued to raid houses and make arrests during the three-day trial run for this in March, now they backed off. We didn't know it, but the leaders of the IRA travelled to London to meet Whitelaw and to demand a British withdrawal from Ireland. With both wings of the IRA now on ceasefire, it seemed really possible that the troubles were over.

On the last day before the ceasefire, we reported the violence in the run-up to it and the doubts over its prospects.

*Bomb Blast Wrecks Pig Testing Centre.*
*Child Shot as Gunman Fires on Army Patrol.*
*Provo Splinter Group to Break Truce.*

A major assumption behind the fear that breakaway Provos would wreck the truce was that the Provo leadership wanted the truce to work. The men suspected of leading a breakaway faction were jail-breakers Martin Meehan and Dutch Doherty with Leo Martin. *The Sunday News* had reported three months earlier, paradoxically, that Doherty had been kicked out of the IRA because he *wanted* a truce. It attributed the new story to 'both Provisional and Official IRA sources in Dublin'.

The sacked Prime Minister of Northern Ireland, Brian Faulkner, said that he had 'no faith at all' in the coming ceasefire. He was off to the US, according to our report, to argue in the media there for a 'plebiscite among the Irish people'. That seems very unlikely indeed. No unionist would have wanted any legitimacy accorded to the majority view of the people of the island of Ireland. This story was probably extracted from agency copy filed by a reporter who simply didn't understand that Ireland was partitioned. Leslie must have been half-asleep when he subbed it. The reporter asked Mr Faulkner if he was optimistic about peace and an end to terrorism. He said: 'It all depends on how "unconditional" this ceasefire really is.'

*The Sunday News* had more faith than Faulkner. An article about the 220 unsolved murders in Northern Ireland said: 'Most of them were the work of the Provisional IRA during the campaign which is scheduled to end tomorrow night.'

But if the Provos were planning to end their campaign, for what gain were their members still risking death and imprisonment on the streets on the eve of the ceasefire?

At the end of the first week of the ceasefire, the paper was reporting that the UDA had built new barricades in several areas; these were strong 'permanent' barricades. A picture showed masked men ripping through paving with pneumatic drills. I had a story that hooded men of the Official IRA, who were supposedly on ceasefire too, were patrolling the Markets area in a Land-Rover. They told me:

> This is not a breach of our truce. The army does not come into this area any more so it is up to us, as the army of the people, to protect the people. We will protect them against any aggression, be it the UDA, the Provisionals or the British.

My invitation to ride in the Land-Rover had come after one of the Rosatto boys left a message at my home to say that if I went to the Markets at eight that night there would be a story for me. I didn't know what the story was, so Jim was happy to let me go but not to spare a photographer. I took Marc Crawford, a friend of Stephen's from *Ebony* magazine. Marc attracted amazement wherever he went in Belfast, a city with few black people then. We stood in front of a bar as advised and others gathered around us. Then down the street came the grey Land-Rover with four masked gunmen in it. The crowd cheered and children ran whooping around it when it stopped in front of us. I interviewed the men. They showed me their guns and described them for me. A Luger, a hunting rifle, an M1 Carbine. I took notes.

Marc had a similar strategy to Chris's of making himself

conspicuous to reassure people. He had an ebullient manner and amused everyone by wearing a black beret, standard paramilitary uniform, though no one was going to mistake a black man in Belfast for a local militant. His favourite story went like this: 'I was talking to a woman up the Falls Road and she told me that her son got twenty years for shoplifting. I said, "That's a lot of time for shoplifting." She said, "Well, he did lift it thirty feet off the ground."'

'Would you like a spin?' asked the driver.

Marc and I got on board and the armed Stickies toured the streets in imitation of the frequent British army patrols. What did this say about security? Why hadn't the army intervened? I would have expected them to open fire, but I trusted, at the same time, that these men knew where they were safe and where they were not. It was, after all, just a propaganda exercise and not a very good one since we didn't have a photographer with us. A woman lent Marc a Kodak Instamatic and let him keep the film.

When I got back to the office, I was elated to have a story. 'The police were talking about you on the radio,' said Rick. They had spotted the Land-Rover but held fire because there were 'spooks' on board.

It must have been a strange time to be a soldier in Belfast, watching the rapid carve-up of the city by armed groups and doing nothing to stop it. The security forces had, we reported, obviously been given instructions not to interfere with loyalists barricading Protestant areas and appeared to have preferred not to try to intercept the Land-Rover either.

The story, further down, identified a murder victim found by children on waste ground on the Protestant side of the peace line near the Shankill Road. The kidnappers of Daniel Hayes had tied him up, gagged him, put a hood over his head and shot him. The police had yet to identify another man found hooded and shot dead in Ballygomartin. He would turn out to be Paul Jobling. Jobling and Hayes had both been killed by loyalists. Republicans had committed the first sectarian murder of the ceasefire four days earlier, shooting 18-year-old Bill Galloway in Tiger's Bay.

Still, shop owners were glad, according to *The Sunday News*, that the threat of bombs and incendiaries had been lifted from them. 'Belfast was almost back to normal yesterday as shoppers flocked into the city on the first weekend since the Provisionals' ceasefire.' Mr David Robertson, a director of Anderson and McAuley, said: 'I think it is like old times again. People are actually shopping now as opposed to coming in to buy something specific and getting out of town as quickly as possible.'

However, there were strange ways in which life had been improved, at least for some, by the tension and violence. The troubles had reduced the suicide rate but increased road deaths. Even in 1972, we saw a close inverse relationship between murder and suicide. The paper reported that 70 people had killed themselves in Northern Ireland in 1965, before the troubles. 'From then until 1968 — when the total was ninety-nine — the figure steadily climbed. In 1969, ninety-two people took their own lives. The following year it was sixty: the figure in 1971 was even lower, fifty-two.'

Another story of unforeseen social consequences quoted the NSPCC saying that there were fewer social problems now in Portadown. NSPCC inspector Adam Turner said his caseload was halved by violence. People were 'getting rid of their hatred in other ways, through fighting.'

The ceasefires did not bring peace; they changed the pattern of violence. Loyalist groups escalated their attacks more sharply than ever before. From the beginning of the troubles to the start of the ceasefire, loyalist gunmen had killed 22 people. They killed 14 others in the bombing of McGurk's Bar. Through the shootings, they were accumulating experience in close-up assassination. They killed another eight during the ceasefire and 21 in the whole

Journalists were barred from commenting on Bloody Sunday once the Widgery Tribunal was established, but Martyn Turner got away with it impugning the judge's integrity.
(© Martyn Turner)

William Craig must have felt like the most important man in Northern Ireland when he summoned his Vanguard followers around him, but he didn't fulfil his promise to them.
(© Victor Patterson)

The horrific Máire Drumm urges the IRA to keep bombing. (© Victor Patterson)

An early UDA barricade as the loyalists organise for civil war.
(© Victor Patterson)

Stephen in the ruins of North Street after an IRA bomb.

Marc Crawford and me on North Street.

A loyalist cartoon shows they understood why the IRA was losing so many bombers and killing so many civilians. They weren't giving the bomb teams access to the bomb timers.

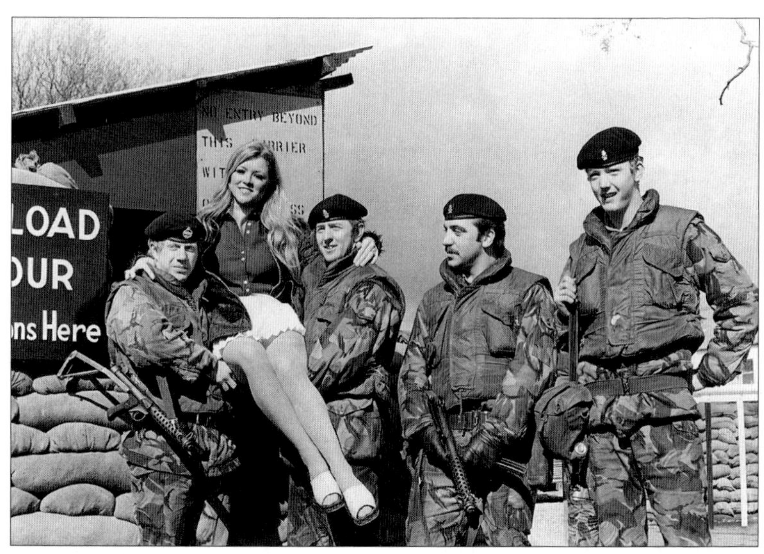


Susan Doughtrey. The army hired glamour girls to cheer up the troops, and invited the press in to record the occasion. (© Victor Patterson)

The loyalists apparently had a sense of humour, even back then.

The secretary of state, William Whitelaw, briefly imagined that, in the spring of 1972, he could reconcile the competing claims on him. The summer would prove him wrong. (© Martyn Turner)

E.R:

TOP SECRET

COPY NO 6 of 6

Prime Minister

NOTE OF A MEETING WITH REPRESENTATIVES OF THE PROVISIONAL IRA

On the instructions of the Secretary of State I met representatives of the Provisional IRA at 3 pm on Tuesday, 20 June. The meeting took place at Ballyarnett, a house near the Donegal border owned by Colonel M W McCorkell. The Colonel and Mrs McCorkell were in the house at the time.

2. The IRA representatives were Mr David O'Connell and Mr Gerard Adams. I was accompanied by Mr Frank Steele.

3. Before the discussions proper started I was introduced to a third person, Mr P J McGrory who was described as a solicitor and a wholly independent person. It had been arranged that I should carry with me a note signed by the Secretary of State to say that I was an authorised representative. This note is in the following terms:

> "The bearer of this note, Mr P J Woodfield, is a senior official in my Department. He has full authority to explain my position on the three points which have been put to me.
>
> He is being accompanied by Mr Steele, another official in my Department.
>
> (signed) William Whitelaw
> Secretary of State
> for Northern Ireland"

Mr McGrory's function appeared to be to scrutinise this note and by virtue of his legal powers he pronounced it authentic and then withdrew.

4. We began the meeting with a statement from me outlining the position of the Provisional IRA as reported to the Secretary of State which was as follows:

> The IRA were prepared to call an indefinite cease fire if they could be satisfied that the Secretary of State would accept the demand of certain convicted prisoners for "political status"; that he would immediately order the cessation of all harassment of the IRA; and that he would be prepared after the cease fire had been shown to be effective to meet representatives of the Provisional IRA.

TOP SECRET

P.J. Woodfield's record of his secret meeting with IRA delegates Gerry Adams and Daithí Ó Conaill.

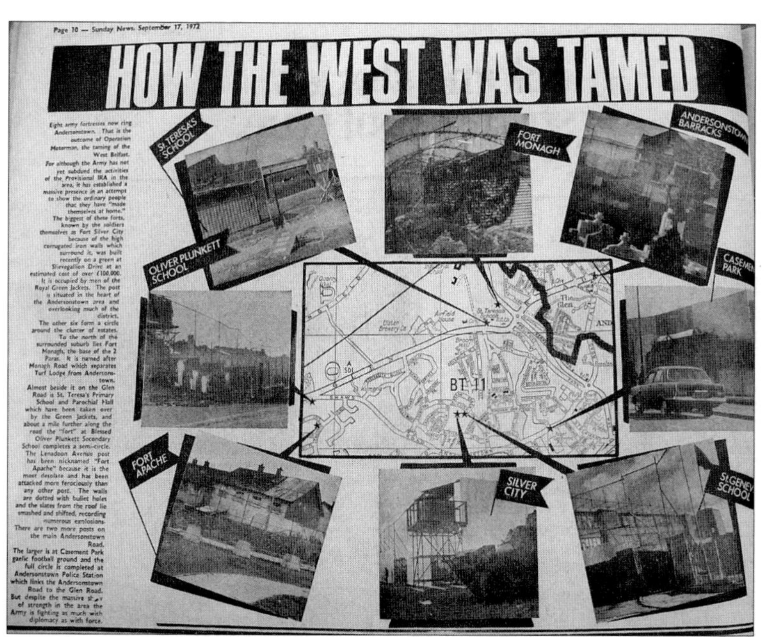

Page 10 — Sunday News, September 17, 1972

# HOW THE WEST WAS TAMED

Eight army fortresses now ring Andersonstown. That is the outcome of Operation Motorman, the taming of the West Belfast.

For although the Army has not yet subdued the activities of the Provisional IRA in the area, it has established a massive presence in an attempt to show the ordinary people that they have "made themselves at home."

The biggest of these forts, known by the soldiers themselves as Fort Silver City because of the high corrugated iron walls which surround it, was built recently on a green at Slievegallion Drive at an estimated cost of over £100,000.

It is occupied by men of the Royal Green Jackets. The post is situated in the heart of the Andersonstown area and overlooking much of the district.

The other six form a circle around the cluster of estates.

To the north of the surrounded suburb lies Fort Monagh, the base of the 2 Paras. It is named after Monagh Road which separates Turf Lodge from Andersonstown.

Almost beside it on the Glen Road is St. Teresa's Primary School and Parochial Hall which have been taken over by the Green Jackets, and about a mile further along the road the "fort" at Blessed Oliver Plunkett Secondary School completes a semi-circle.

The Lenadoon Avenue post has been nicknamed "Fort Apache" because it is the most desolate and has been attacked more ferociously than any other post. The walls are dotted with bullet holes and the slates from the roof lie smashed and shifted, recording numerous explosions.

There are two more posts on the main Andersonstown Road.

The larger is at Casement Park gaelic football ground and the full circle is completed at Andersonstown Police Station which links the Andersonstown Road to the Glen Road.

But despite the massive show of strength in the area the Army is fighting as much with diplomacy as with force.



My report on the surrounding of Andersonstown after Operation Motorman.

Kelly's Cellars, the pub where reporters felt safe, because paramilitaries drank there too.

of July 1972 — as many as from the start of the troubles to then. Either a small number of people were gaining extensive experience in close-quarter murder or many were out killing for the first time.

It was in May, weeks before the ceasefires, that the loyalist killings had begun to increase in frequency. In April, loyalists killed two Catholics, randomly selected. One of them was Sean McConville, shot in Ardoyne by Protestants in a car. Stephen and I went out to the scene immediately afterwards, and found a quiet spring Saturday evening. People were having their tea before going out to the pub. At this stage, there was little context in which to set such a killing.

In May, loyalists had killed ten people, some of them just picked up by trawling gun gangs and shot on the street. By the time of the Provo ceasefire, these killings were routine, though not as frequent as killings by the IRA. So the ceasefire did not promise perfect peace and it was soon clear that the IRA, while on ceasefire, would still reserve the right to kill civilians, both Protestant and Catholic. In fact, it was not peace at all that was on offer but a phase in which the violence looked less like a liberation struggle against British forces and more like a murky war between Protestants and Catholics, in which each side punished the other by killing randomly captured people in ones and twos. It was against this background of murder that the British government sat down to talk to the IRA.

The Provisionals set up roadblocks in Catholic areas in imitation of the British army and, in further imitation of them, even shot dead two drivers who crashed through them, Bernard Norney in Ballymurphy and Samuel Robinson in Cavendish Street. When loyalist gangs killed Catholics and dumped their bodies on waste ground in Westway Drive, republicans (Provisional or Official) shot two random Protestants and dumped their bodies on waste ground off the Cliftonville Road. Then loyalists killed another two

Catholics and then another one and then two Protestant boys, for reasons that are not clear.

In a two-week ceasefire, the loyalist and republican groups killed 16 people between them. At a death rate of more than one a day, it was one of the busiest fortnights of the whole troubles for all groups, though not nearly as bad as the fortnight to follow.

This was the precedent for the type of ceasefire that would be accepted by governments years later. How would we know that the paramilitaries were on ceasefire? They would tell us. They would be the sole arbiters of it. So long as they didn't attack the army or the police, or bomb commercial property, the governments would accept as a basis for negotiation any cessation, however qualified, no matter how many ordinary people were killed.

# Chapter 23

The Provisional IRA ended its ceasefire over a dispute about its plans to move Catholics into vacant houses, formerly occupied by Protestants, in lower Lenadoon estate on the western edge of Belfast. But this was just an excuse. The negotiations on a truce had already been held in London. The Secretary of State, William Whitelaw, had met the IRA leadership at Paul Channon's house in Cheyne Walk. The IRA had delivered its demand for British withdrawal from Ireland, and Whitelaw had determined that this was an impossible demand to meet. 'Absurd' he later called it. So the purpose of the ceasefire had been met.

The two sides had come together and confirmed that there was no basis for an agreement between them. Both must have known that the ceasefire would now end. Those of us who looked on really believed, because the IRA wanted us to believe it, that if the army let the families through to Horn Drive, the ceasefire would continue. It would not have continued. Another breaking point would have been chosen. The army and Whitelaw must have known this. The gunmen were in place.

The last day of the ceasefire was 9 July. The paper was

aware by then of extraordinary relations between the British army and the paramilitaries. A photograph on the front page appeared to show British soldiers inspecting UDA men on parade. The caption explained that it was not quite like that: 'it just so happened that members of the UDA were manning a barricade at the top of the Castlereagh Road, Belfast, yesterday when an Army foot patrol passed by.'

However, the lead story concerned a wholly changed relationship between the army and the IRA, and reported that senior army officers had had a tense meeting with the Provo leadership.

> The secret meeting was held in the heavily fortified army post in Lenadoon Avenue which sits in a tense no man's land between the predominantly Protestant Horn Drive estate on one side and the Catholic Lenadoon estate on the other.

The IRA was telling the army that it intended to move 16 Catholic families into houses allocated to them in Horn Drive, though the UDA had pledged to prevent this. Gangs with cudgels had been bussed into the area and were waiting for an IRA order to move towards Horn Drive.

> Later, four well-known IRA leaders, including one man who has been described as the most wanted fugitive in Northern Ireland at the present time, walked quickly from the post and climbed into a car which roared up Lenadoon Avenue towards the Catholic district.

The report didn't say who had described this unnamed man as 'the most wanted fugitive in Northern Ireland at the present time' nor explain why he couldn't be named. Presumably it was a reference to either Seamus Twomey or Joe Cahill. The army and the IRA had agreed to extend the deadline for moving the families until four o'clock on the

Sunday, the afternoon of the day that paper was published.

> Republican sources hinted that the army officers involved in the secret negotiations were trying to arrange a meeting between the 'leaders of the Catholic community' and the Secretary of State for Northern Ireland, Mr William Whitelaw.

What the paper didn't know was that a meeting between the IRA leaders and William Whitelaw had already taken place and that the IRA delegation at that meeting had included those with authority in Lenadoon. And a liaison had already been established between the IRA and the Northern Ireland Office through which IRA complaints about army behaviour could be relayed to the government.

With Northern Ireland descending into chaos, *The Sunday News* then chose to divert two pages of the paper every week for the summer to the life of the comedian Terry-Thomas, starting that week. Terry-Thomas would get more space than the bloodiest events of that summer, and more than the most intriguing and challenging political crises. Perhaps the editor had bought serialisation rights in anticipation of an uneventful summer. For the next five weeks, in the most tumultuous time in Northern Ireland's history, two full pages of each issue would be devoted to the life of Terry-Thomas, as if it were just as important to us as the deepening crisis.

And I had a nice article in this issue about the Divine Light Mission ashram in Belfast. One of Guru Maharaji's mahatmas had come to Belfast, and the devotees told me that for the 22 hours that he was in Northern Ireland, all violence had ceased.

I was in Lenadoon Avenue, watching the lorry with household furniture drive to the army barrier. It was a bright sunny July afternoon. I didn't need to be there. Our paper was out. This was a day off. Hundreds of people filled the street. They were not in an organised parade. They just knew that big things were about to happen. Many of the houses across the top of Lenadoon Avenue had riflemen at their front windows. One team had a Lewis gun. One of the men handling it had broken the window with the gun to set it in position and had been told off by others for imposing so roughly on the hospitality of the people.

The furniture lorry approached the barrier. The crowd turned to watch and cheer. Seamus Twomey negotiated with the army. This was a formality. The main talking was finished now and Twomey was merely confirming what he already knew, that they were not getting through. That done, he turned, as arranged, to Tommy Gorman, and said: 'It's over.' Gorman signalled to the riflemen at the windows. And suddenly the air was alive with gunfire and we were all running. I ran into a garden and scrambled around to the back of the house, through another hedge, into a deserted street. I didn't know the area well. There was another loud rip from a submachine gun. If I was seen dashing across open ground, I might be taken for a target. I wondered if I had been wise to leave the main crowd, but the crowd would probably have fragmented by now too.

I walked home with the sound of gunfire, sometimes faint and sometimes awfully close, depending on how the wind gusted, or perhaps on the echo from Black Mountain behind me. At home, I sat tremulous with horror, looking into a ghastly and pointless future in which this mayhem would never go away. I was morose with disappointment. I wanted out. I had wanted the ceasefire to work. I did not know what was clear later, that the IRA had devised a breakdown to facilitate a return to war on terms that it expected its own community base would accept. The IRA could hardly have come back from talks in London and told us: the British have refused our demand that they leave Ireland, so we have no choice but to continue the killing. At least, their own calculation at that time was that they could not have done it that way. It was already clear that few Catholics would accept the demand for a united Ireland as a basis for war but that more would accept that the Provisionals had been drawn into war by repression and bad politics.

One of the people shooting that day was Billy the thief.

'I was firing in the air with a Tommy gun and praying that I didn't hit anybody,' he said.

I didn't want to know. If I had been thinking like a real journalist, I would have pleaded with him for a full account, of course.

Those who died that day, strangely, were not shot in Lenadoon. Nobody died there. Usually nobody did die in a well-planned gun battle. Most of the carnage of that evening happened miles away in Springhill. The first to die there, John Dougal, was a 16-year-old IRA man. The army claimed to have exchanged fire with him but no forensic traces were found on him to suggest he had held a weapon. Another of those to die was a priest, Fr Noel Fitzpatrick. He had been praying over one of the others, 13-year-old Margaret Gargan. The bullet that passed through him killed Patrick Butler.

A 14-year-old member of the Official IRA, Dean McCafferty, was hit and killed while trying to drag Fr Fitzpatrick's body to safety. Had there been a gun battle there too, I thought, it must have been much worse than the one at Lenadoon, and yet that one had been terrible. The army and police said that there had been a fierce gun battle in Springhill, between Paratroopers based at Corry's woodyard and local Provisionals. The IRA and local people said that there had been no attack by the IRA in Springhill, that civilians on the street had been shot at by loyalist or army snipers in the woodyard. The army later claimed to have identified precise targets and not to have been just reacting to shots reverberating across the mountain from Lenadoon.

Jim sent me to Springhill to try to get the story of the

cluster of killings there. I called at the Whiterock Tenants' Association. Frank Cahill, the brother of the IRA leader Joe Cahill, took me through the streets to the place where each victim had fallen, and showed me that each spot was overlooked by J.P. Corry's big timber yard. His theory was that British soldiers had let loyalist gunmen into the yard to select random Catholic targets on the street. It is generally accepted now that soldiers fired those shots themselves. The army claimed that it was returning fire on identified gunmen.

We didn't use the story. I don't know why. Perhaps there was a risk of libelling the owners of the timber yard or perhaps Frank Cahill's claim that the army was working with the loyalists was too flimsy to found a story on. Cahill had pointed out little rectangular openings in the wall of the timber yard and claimed that these were the sniping positions. I would have had to go in and see them from the other side before quoting a claim like that. But instead of taking more time to look into it, we dropped it.

Five people dead, apparently murdered: the army's retaliation against the IRA for ending the ceasefire? And yet these deaths seemed to dissolve out of detail into the background of killing, to be ultimately no more distinctive than any of the others.

# Chapter 24

If the media had little sense of what the IRA was thinking as it entered the ceasefire, what about the British intelligence services? We have an insight available now in the report of P.J. Woodfield, the British diplomat who met two IRA leaders, Daithí Ó Conaill and Gerry Adams, to negotiate the terms of the 1972 ceasefire. Woodfield wrote his account of his meeting with the IRA delegation at a time when it was still possible to believe that the leaders were genuinely interested in a long-term peace. He was himself persuaded that Adams and Ó Conaill wanted an end to living on the run. Adams told him that he would like to go to university. 'We are not stopping you,' said Woodfield. But how must Woodfield have read the intentions of these two men when it became clear that the IRA did not want a long ceasefire?

His account of his meeting with Ó Conaill and Adams depicts them as fundamentally decent but perhaps naïve political operators who had to be corrected by him, over and over again, on what were the limits of the possible. If, as seems likely, Adams and Ó Conaill knew that the IRA had no intention of ending its war, their feints and probes through the diplomatic austerity of P.J. Woodfield have to be understood differently. We don't know how he reflected on them, himself, a month later. We have to reach back through time, and tap that man on the shoulder and suggest that Ó Conaill and Adams are not to be judged as peacemakers at all but as deft warriors with a repertoire of traps primed for him.

The meeting was planned as a response to three questions put to the British government by the IRA: would prisoners be given political status?; in the event of a ceasefire, would the British army cease its harassment of the IRA?; and how soon, after a ceasefire was declared, would the Secretary of State be willing to meet the IRA leadership?

The two sides were laying down preparations for an IRA meeting with Whitelaw. What did P.J. Woodfield expect the IRA would want out of that meeting? If the IRA was negotiating for political status for the prisoners, why not then for a complete amnesty? Perhaps because political status would be an asset to them through a long campaign, an amnesty only at the end of it, and they did not expect it to be ending. The British appear not to have considered this. They probably just thought the naïve Provos were being cautiously modest in their demands, which they have never been.

The first of the three questions had been answered before the meeting. On the previous day, prisoners at Crumlin Road jail had called off a hunger strike for political status, satisfied with concessions made to them which accorded them Special Category Status. Adams and Ó Conaill affected not to know about this in order to lay their first trap for Woodfield. He should, they said, phone the jail and demand that the Governor bring an IRA leader to the phone to speak to them.

Woodfield refused, since this would compromise the secrecy of the talks.

Woodfield saw the danger and averted it but he did not seriously consider that this request cast doubt on the sincere desire of Adams and Ó Conaill to make the ceasefire plan work.

The IRA delegates sought to test the government's influence with the UDA. Would the Northern Ireland Office be prepared to introduce the IRA leaders to the UDA? The IRA might get along a lot better with them than the government would expect, they said. Woodfield's answer is not recorded but had he then approached the UDA to set up such a meeting, he would surely have inflamed the violence further. Imagine a leader of the UDA being summoned to the Northern Ireland Office to be told that there was a nice man from the IRA who would like to meet him. The secret negotiations with the IRA would have been disclosed to the violent force most likely to protest against them. Was that a sign of naïveté on the part of the IRA or a deft manoeuvre to tip the British into embarrassment and chaos? Woodfield read it as naïveté.

Every time the IRA was faced with a request to recognise British difficulty, it opted for the least sensitive response, yet the manner of Adams and Ó Conaill was construed by Woodfield as obliging and amenable. Asked to leave MacStíofáin off the delegation and to keep the delegation small, the IRA included MacStíofáin and most of the senior leadership. Given to believe that it would be difficult for the government to commit itself to allowing the IRA members, during the ceasefire, to carry guns, the delegation brought a gun with them to the meeting with Whitelaw. Woodfield explained to them that he would like there to be two weekends within the ten-day period of the ceasefire before the meeting with Whitelaw could take place; the IRA timed the ceasefire to start on a Monday for no apparent reason other than to deny him this.

And crucially, though Woodfield had understood that the ceasefire included avoidance of conflict with loyalists, the IRA entered into a tit-for-tat war with the loyalists. Advised that the army would play a low-key role but could not accept IRA guidelines on areas to stay out of, the IRA set up checkpoints in Catholic areas to assert itself as the legitimate army presence there.

All these moves would have had meaning for the British in terms of Woodfield's discussion. They were all symbolic denials of any ground to the British. Adams and Ó Conaill had located points of anxiety and, instead of working with the British by assuaging those anxieties, in all cases they aggravated them. The British must have known that they were being toyed with and virtually challenged to disqualify the ceasefire as grounds for talks. Woodfield must have wondered afterwards if he had been hoodwinked by the 'respectable and respectful' Mr Adams and Mr Ó Conaill.

The reality, on reflection, appears to be that the Provisionals had intimated their desire for a ceasefire, and played along with the mediators, in order to placate a clear demand from the Catholic community that they should stop their armed campaign, and also to achieve political status for the prisoners. They came out of the ceasefire with a good excuse for breaking it, which appeared to confirm British support for loyalists, and they had even secured effective political status before the ceasefire started. These were good results for a paramilitary army that had, three months earlier, been faced with enormous pressure to cut its losses and give up.

However, the media had not understood this strategy, indeed had no access to Woodfield's report until 30 years later. We now have no better insight into the psychology and strategy of the Provisional IRA at that time than Woodfield's report read against the events that immediately followed it. The people controlling events best to their own advantage and programme were the Provisionals.

# Part Five

# Chapter 25

Stephen came in one day with his arm bandaged.

'Don't tell me now that we don't need the British forces in Ulster,' he said.

'What happened to you?'

'Malachi, I wouldn't be here but for the soldiers.' He tossed what looked like a piece of bent brass across the desk to me.

'Uh?'

'A bullet; an actual, spent, copper-jacketed 7.62 army bullet.'

This story didn't go into the paper.

'The woman up the street from me keeps — kept — a big Alsatian dog. And she was torturing it when she got drunk for the Twelfth and it turned on her.

'I was in the house and I heard all this shrieking and barking and ran out. The dog was going for her. There was blood everywhere. You've never seen anything like it. So I was trying to pull the dog off her and these Welsh soldiers turned up. A foot patrol. And one of them was going to shoot the dog and I was shouting at him, "Don't!" Then the dog turned round on me and sank its teeth in my arm.'

We were all aghast. What a story!

'Then he shot the dog.'

'Shot the dog?'

'Shot the fucking dog. So I don't want to hear any more Brits-out crap.'

'Did the head just blow out?' I was thinking of the photographs of the two women shot in the car in Raglan Street.

'No, the first bullet just seemed to make him stagger a bit, went through the body and took the wind out of him. The second finished him.'

'And I suppose', said Jim, 'if the UVF had shot the dog, you'd be singing their praises too?'

'No Brits — no Stephen. Simple as that.'

Stephen got to know that soldier and even had him over to tea, though never on the same night that I was there. His name was Brian Kelly. Stephen wrote to the General Officer Commanding, Lieutenant General Sir Harry Tuzo, to tell him how much he appreciated his men shooting the dog. Tuzo wrote back:

> I am delighted that you have taken the trouble to write such an appreciative letter, and I am sure that the 1st Bn Royal Regiment of Wales will be equally sustained by your gesture. I can tell you that it is a pleasant change to receive such a despatch, and much preferable to some of the complaining letters I receive.

There were other occasions also when lives were saved by available guns, including the guns of the IRA. My brother Roger had got off a bus from the city centre one evening at Finaghy crossroads. We had been aware throughout childhood that there was some risk of being accosted or abused when we went to Finaghy, a Protestant area, but, even in the early 1970s, this risk was not enough to deter us from using the route altogether.

A group of young Protestants had been waiting on the

railway bridge to pick a target from among all those walking north towards Riverdale. They selected Roger and his friend and tried to grab hold of them. It would be a long run to safety. Roger turned into a small housing estate and was cornered. He beat at the door of a house, pleading to be let in, but the Protestants had him on the ground and were kicking him and lashing at him with a chain while he cowered and covered himself, and took the blows on his hands and arms.

His friend had put his faith in his feet and had run straight on up Finaghy Road North and into Riverdale. He came around the corner into our street, shouting to the men at the barricade that the prods had got Roger O'Doherty and were killing him. It was lucky that the men of E Company usually didn't have far to reach for their weapons. They ran down Finaghy Road North, shooting in the air. That scared off Roger's attackers. If there had been no IRA there, Roger would have been killed. But if there had been no IRA at all, he perhaps wouldn't have been attacked in the first place.

My family suffered no great loss through the worst of the troubles yet all of us encountered life-threatening danger. The difference between us and many others is that we survived and they did not. We got over it and they left behind bereaved and stricken relatives who still think about their loss every day.

Barney, my father, worked in a bar on the Oldpark Road, in north Belfast. Loyalists planted a bomb in the doorway one night and a child came in and told them it was there. The whole crowd scrambled to get out, leaping over the bomb into the street. Barney, coming from behind the bar, was among the last to get out over the bomb. He watched his panicking customers flee down a hallway to the door, knowing that, at any second, the bomb might blow bits of them back over him.

He jumped over the bomb in turn. A man's balls must feel

particularly vulnerable in a leap like that. He got into the street and away before the bomb exploded and demolished the bar. He had parked his car outside. The bomb smashed the side windows of the car and he had no choice but to drive it home that night, with bits of glass littering the seats and the floor. And because he was a dramatic and expressive man who had tired us with his tempers, we sympathised but guarded ourselves against having to hear his story over and over again.

'Och,' said Maguire, with a poor joke, 'you should have known not to park your car near a likely target like that.'

Barney leapt up at him and grabbed him by the throat. Very embarrassing. 'Get out of my house.'

'He was right,' said Maguire later. 'He was entitled to more sympathy.'

At home in Riverdale, the gunmen were out of the known safe houses and asking their neighbours for sofas to sleep on, spreading the risk. People who had no real sympathy for the IRA lay awake at night, listening to young men cleaning their weapons downstairs, coming upstairs to use their bathrooms. I had answered the door to two teenagers. 'Barney said we could stay here.'

Perhaps he hadn't had much choice. Mum, behind me, called out, 'That's all right.'

'No guns,' I said, but no one was going to heed what I said.

I let them in, but I lay in bed that night, listening to their coming and going. Others joined them. There was a rattle of submachine gunfire out on Finaghy Road North and they let themselves in, and the house was filled with the smell of burnt cordite. In the morning, I looked into the kitchen where four of them were making breakfast and I decided to leave. I would stay with Fegan or Stephen on those nights when E Company had the use of my home.

A few days later, Mum told me that she had found a pistol

under a cushion on the living-room sofa and had taken it back to Tucker Kane, who had apologised and assured her that it was only a dummy, whatever that meant. People arrested in house searches that turned up guns at that time were getting sentences of 14 years and the shite kicked out of them too. The danger of that happening to me had just risen too sharply to be tolerable.

The ceasefire experiment was over and the British had nothing to show for it, except perhaps a clearer understanding of the intentions and methods of the IRA. The IRA resumed its bombings and attacks on the police and army. The army, no longer restrained by ceasefire terms, entered the ghetto areas in strength. Republicans contested this most effectively in the Lenadoon area, where they had crashed the ceasefire. On 16 July, a week after that breakdown, *The Sunday News* reported that dozens of families had left their homes in Lenadoon in protest against the army's occupation of flat blocks there. These people believed that this occupation had drawn fire from the IRA.

I was in Lenadoon on the next Saturday night and walked around the area. There were reporters from Britain and America there, too. I walked along the Glen Road near the top of Ramoan Gardens, past the school I had gone to. It was a lovely July night. A motor bike went past with two men on it. There was a sudden rip of automatic fire from somewhere, perhaps from the motorbike. I dived into fresh-cut grass. There was more distant gunfire too. Everyone was waiting and there was a strangely carnival atmosphere, as there always was when all other concerns were overwhelmed. My job was simply to stay in the area and phone in details that Jim and the others could write up. Jim drew on other sources too, including the Official IRA, officially on ceasefire still. The Officials claimed they had 'been in action several times in the past week ... in defence of the working-class people.'

On the Sunday, hundreds gathered on the Shaw's Road to

march to Casement Park football ground a mile away, for a protest rally against the army occupation of Lenadoon. They said they would not go back to their homes. In the evening, some did, and some camped in a local school.

There was a funny moment at the rally itself when one of the speakers, Paddy Kennedy, said that they would be ending now so that people could get to evening mass. This was before the days when Catholics were allowed to attend a Sunday Mass on a Saturday night. 'Some fucking revolution this,' said a man behind me, 'when the priest says we're to shut up and go down to the church.'

One night, I met Gerry O'Hare and Jimmy Drumm. They were driving around the area in a black Ford Zephyr, the sort of car a priest would use. They took me to the school they had occupied, to see the remaining Lenadoon refugees there. Gerry was annoyed that two armed men had been posted at the gates of the school, and asked Jimmy who had put them there. Jimmy said he would get them stood down.

We then went to the home of Tom Conaty, a local man who had faced protests from the IRA at his home, for accepting an appointment to an advisory committee serving the Secretary of State. At one in the morning, these two members of IRA brigade staff and I sat in Mr Conaty's living room while they reported to him conditions as they saw them. At no time did they tell him that I was a reporter, so he must have assumed that I was either a very senior Provo myself or that I was their bodyguard.

Some secret link between Whitelaw and the IRA was represented by this meeting, and the IRA was wilfully compromising it by having me there. I wrote nothing about it. I wasn't confident enough that I understood the game in play.

In the same week that I was getting this insight into the high politics of conflict management, I wrote a story about a war breaking out between local hippies. I was as unsure of what to believe about the one conflict as about the other. The hippy war story came from Terri Hoolly, whom I had known on and off for a couple of years. Terri published small magazines, wore his hair long and addressed me as 'man'. I called at his flat on Cromwell Road one morning and discovered him still in bed, on a mattress on the floor of a cluttered room. I didn't know if Terri lived in a fantasy world or the real one, but I wasn't sure which one I was living in myself either. The story he told seemed grotesque and implausible. A group of Freaks for Ulster had declared war on other freaks for their 'apathy and indifference' to the troubles. They had tried to burn the flat of 'a rival hippy tribe leader'.

Freaks for Ulster had sent Terri Hoolly a letter, saying that they were 'keeping tabs on him'. I quoted Terri saying: 'I know it must sound very much like a joke but I am not laughing.'

It had been 'another busy week for the gravediggers' said one of our columnists, Observer. He had counted 22 known civilians and six British soldiers killed since the end of the ceasefire. 'Today the Provisional IRA stands exposed as the greatest scourge ever inflicted on innocent and helpless Irishmen and women.'

In fact, 35 people died in that week, but Observer had had to get his copy in early. Of that 35, twelve had been killed by the British army and five by loyalists, so the IRA had indeed been the 'greatest scourge' but not the only one.

# Chapter 26

Now that the Provos had rejected the political overtures of the government and undermined Whitelaw's hopes of incorporating them into a political settlement, they sought to force him into taking military measures which they would also show were worthless. That is, I believe, what Bloody Friday was for.

Eddie and I were walking up Royal Avenue on a bright July lunchtime. He was an amateur photographer and had advised me on cameras and equipment to buy. We stopped to browse in shop windows and I saw a suede jacket I fancied. I had nothing like it. It was a trim jacket with a zip and breast pockets, and I was thin enough then to wear one like that. I went in and tried it on, and immediately wrote a cheque for it and came back out onto the street feeling pleased with myself. Then we heard a bomb go off. That wasn't unusual, but it was less likely at that time of day. And why would anyone in their right mind want to ruin a lovely summer's afternoon?

We walked back to the office and heard another explosion on the way. Then another. A column of smoke snaked into the sky to the east of us. There were sirens. And there was a tangible anxiety in the air. Those who have lived through those days probably feel that if they went back in a time machine, they could identify 1972 by that tension. Even journalism referred to 'increasing tension in Belfast', though readers and listeners in London or Dublin probably didn't realise that this described a kind of a psychic charge that spoiled everything, from the taste of your food to the fit of your clothes.

Inside the newspaper building, everyone was going down into the print room for shelter. One of the girls was shrieking and had to be helped to walk. She kept sinking to her knees. I had often joked with her when we passed on the stairs and had never thought that I would see her in the throes of panic. Someone explained that she had survived a bomb attack at the Milk Marketing Board before coming to work at the newspaper. We all stood and waited. 'It's like the Blitz,' said Paddy.

'Are you okay?' asked one of the reporters from another office. I must have looked frightened. I didn't want to look frightened. I stayed close to Paddy, Rick and Eddie. Rick looked up at the high ceiling of the print room and I followed his cynical gaze. The roof was made mostly of glass, one of those serrated factory roofs with skylights. 'If a bomb goes off here, this is the last place we should be.'

'Shouldn't we say something?'

'And cause a panic? Odds are we won't be hit. They can't bomb everyone.'

The IRA bombed 21 targets before it was over and we were back in our office. Jim phoned: 'I got caught in a bomb on the Cavehill Road. I'm okay. It blew me across the street. If my wife phones, don't mention it. Say I'm on my way into the office. I'll call her when I get there. What about the rest of you?'

I was wondering if the shop that sold me the jacket might have been bombed too. Then my cheque might have been destroyed and I would have the jacket for free. The shop survived.

After work, I went to Kelly's Cellars. The bombings were reported on the television news there, with grotesque pictures of death and injury, all overlaid with the sombre tone of the presenter. Some of the men in the cubicles started laughing and mocking the report. I was home by seven on Bloody Friday. It was a good day to be safe by your fireside; the killing was not over yet. My own thoughts were dark and sullen; I was sickened by fear and disgust and deeply confused about where to turn now. I did not enjoy living at home and should have moved out before this. I was quarrelling too often with my father and getting into a habit of drinking after work and coming home drunk and in a sour mood. The last thing a sullen and drunken man needs is a good reason to be angry.

My father had driven to the hospital to collect Mum who was on day shifts now. He came into the living room ahead of her. 'Your mother has cut her finger on the car door. Is there a plaster?'

I said: 'That was bloody lovely today, wasn't it?'

'Oh give over. I have more important things on my mind right now.'

'More important than....'

But he was right; some things are more important than refreshing an endless quarrel between a father and a son.

Our paper, two days after Bloody Friday, led with the 'Crackdown on the IRA'. A second lead at the top of the page reported the previous day's bombing in Armagh, 'as the Provisional IRA kept up their fierce attacks on commercial life in the province.'

Far from being subdued by the carnage of Bloody Friday, the IRA had maintained its momentum, bombing Armagh city centre, blowing up the home of the Earl Castlestewart near Coalisland, bombing Newtownbutler in County Tyrone, bombing Shaw's Bridge in Belfast and opening fire on soldiers across Barnett's Park. The bombers had not been deterred by civilian casualties in Belfast the previous day. We quoted an army spokesman: 'This was obviously an attempt to recreate the horror in Belfast on Friday.' The paper speculated that the 'crackdown against IRA strongholds' represented a 'get tough initiative' which 'could lead to the invasion of the Bogside and Creggan in Derry.'

Mr Whitelaw now said that the Provisionals had been given every opportunity to end violence.

> They have proved that they are determined to wreck Northern Ireland in order to gain their objectives. They must fail. On behalf of Her Majesty's Government, I tell you now, they will fail.

The paper described how army bulldozers had smashed barricades in Andersonstown and young men over 15 were rounded up and checked by Special Branch officers. Those absolved had had their hands stamped with indelible ink and were allowed to go home. The IRA claimed that its Belfast OC had escaped the invasion of Andersonstown, and the Derry IRA was quoted pledging to 'make a last-ditch stand to protect the people of Free Derry' if the army tried to break through the barricades.

Nine people had died in the Bloody Friday bombs, six of them — including two soldiers — at Oxford Street bus station and three on the Cavehill Road, killed by the bomb that had knocked Jim over. We reported on the Sunday that 11 people had been killed in the explosions and that seven had been identified by then. The remaining mass of flesh is now agreed to have made up only two corpses, not four.

'One of the dead was 14-year-old Stephen Parker, son of Rev. Joseph Parker, a chaplain at the Belfast Seamen's Mission.'

We had several eyewitness accounts now.

'It was unbelievable,' said a man who was slightly injured

in the Oxford Street bomb. 'There was a tremendous blast of air and then I was down in the street with these bits of glass around me on the footpath and pieces of flesh and clothing all over and people crying and screaming.'

On that same Friday night, two gunmen had called at the home of the Rosattos. Kevin was in jail at this stage, having been arrested with an M1 carbine, after a gun battle. I hadn't known then that Kevin was a member of the Official IRA. I should have worked it out from an incident one Saturday afternoon in Kelly's. Martin had brought him a drink from the bar, despite his having said that he would sit out that round. Kevin snapped that he was 'under discipline' and could not accept the drink. He poured it out onto the floor.

I liked the Rosatto boys. They were great fun. Martin, who knew I was planning a holiday, taught me to say, '*La guerre, c'est très mauvais.*' This was the line that would impress the French girls, he said.

The gunmen who came to the Rosatto house on the night of Bloody Friday were presumably looking for Martin. His father answered the door. One shot him in the upper leg from about five metres. He died soon after. One theory is that the killers were Provisionals; another is that they were loyalists. Their car had been stolen in the Irish Republic, suggesting republicans, but abandoned in Agnes Street in the Shankill Road area, suggesting loyalists.

Loyalists were definitely responsible for other killings that night. They kidnapped the singer Rose McCartney and her boyfriend Patrick O'Neill and shot them dead, side by side, in a car. The loyalist killers were now at the peak of their campaign. They argued that they were providing defence for their people against the IRA, yet most, nearly all, of their attacks were against random Catholics who crossed their paths.

*The Sunday News* reported all murders on the night of Bloody Friday as the work of 'mystery killers'. It hadn't sunk in yet that the UDA was murdering Catholics, though the paper's report of the deaths described how one of the victims, Francis McArthurs, had been taken out of a taxi, at a barricade, by 'Protestant vigilantes'.

Our chauvinist columnist, Patrick Riddell, was appalled. He saw no political sense in the bombing. 'Well, you Ulster Catholics, those of you who enthusiastically aid and shelter the IRA, are you satisfied? Or do you lust for still more shattered bodies of women and children, murdered in the sacred name of Republican Ireland?'

Later that afternoon, Gerry O'Hare, the IRA Battalion press officer, called up and I answered the phone. 'What the fuck was that all about?' I asked.

'Give me the phone,' said Jim. And he dealt with O'Hare with the ordinary professional mateyness with which we would always speak to press officers in order to get the best out of them. When he had finished, I snapped at Jim: 'Is that what this job demands?'

'If you want them to talk to you, don't start by telling them to fuck off.'

I had a story from home, a scoop. My mother had given it to me. The Provisionals had laid a minefield on waste ground between Riverdale and Finaghy, ostensibly to deter loyalists. I wrote: 'It is believed that an explosives expert was specially brought into Andersonstown for the job and that he is not normally active in the area.' At least, that was the gossip among women who watched the IRA every day from their kitchen windows.

> Riverdale was one of the first Catholic areas of Belfast to be declared 'no-go'. Concrete barricades block all entrances and the only possible way of bringing a car into the area is over a footpath at one of the barricades. This point is patrolled by vigilantes and members of the Provisionals.

My story was picked up by the evening television news.

'How did they find out about that?' said my father.

'Sure aren't there notices up in all the shops,' replied my mother. 'It's hardly a secret.'

But even at such a time, Terry-Thomas got his two-page spread. And a glamour picture showed Pettela Koscielny from Ballynahinch in her bikini on Tyrella Beach. Pettela sat on the bonnet of a car with one leg raised, drinking from a large bottle of lemonade. This picture broke the usual rules about concealing body contours. It had probably been taken by one of our own photographers, rather than the agency which usually supplied the more mannered glamour pics. The caption said that Pettela was 14 years old. If she was that young, the picture would be unusable nowadays, but she looked like a mature woman.

Another report said that Northern Ireland housewives were still buying more butter than margarine, even at times when butter prices were high. 'But things like yoghurt, which are very popular in England, don't sell very well at all in Northern Ireland,' said a city-centre shop manager.

# Chapter 27

You would think that now that the loyalists had entered into their bloodiest phase, the unionists would have been shamed into distancing themselves from the violence, but many continued to rationalise the whole problem as the creation of the IRA.

In September, *The Sunday News* had a story about speculation in a Unionist Party magazine that the killings of Catholics were all the work of the IRA and that there was 'no evidence to suggest that the murder gangs are selectively wiping out Catholics'.

*The Unionist Review* may have been right in the case of Joseph Rosatto, when it claimed that victims of recent murders had been killed in a feud between the Official and Provisional IRA factions. It said that there had been 'an alarming increase in apparently motiveless murders' but that 'the facts [showed] that Catholics [were] no more likely to be killed than Protestants.'

It accused the SDLP of exploiting the murders of Catholics by blaming them on Protestant murder gangs, only in order to bolster up its 'declining prestige'. Aside from being blind to the murdering of Catholics by the UDA, the Ulster Unionist

Party was, effectively, accusing all Catholic victims of having been members of the IRA.

It's not as if the UDA was invisible or its intentions unclear. It was publishing its own papers, like the *WDA* (Woodvale Defence Association), in Protestant areas. For all their pretensions to military dignity and noble purpose, it was often in the smaller, afterthought features, like the letters column, that these papers betrayed their assumption that any Catholic at all was an enemy.

> Dear Sir, I am writing to ask you to print this letter, please.
>
> People think that the Crumlin Cinema is owned by Roman Catholics. This is not true — I work in the Crumlin and have done for 2½ years. The owner's name is Mrs Buckley, and she lives in Lisburn.
>
> Yours sincerely,
>
> (Name and address supplied).

Or:

> *TO WHOM IT MAY CONCERN.*
>
> Mr Kelly, owner of the Solway Wine Stores, Gawn St., is a protestant loyalist, and anything which is rumoured to the contrary will be dealt with by the area commander.

*The Sunday News* published its own research into the killings, with a list of the dead filling a whole page. Some of these killings — or assassinations as they were most commonly called — had been carried out by undercover soldiers of the British army. We got into trouble with the Catholic Ex-Servicemen's Association after that article. The paragraph on Patsy McVeigh described him as 'IRA Catholic'. Patsy McVeigh was the man whose murder had spoiled my grapple with Geraldine. Paddy, who compiled the story, denied that he had used that phrase at all. It wasn't normal usage anyway.

It appears that it was inserted by a mischievous compositor. But a man who was in the IRA at the time says that Patsy McVeigh was, in fact, an 'auxiliary' — that is, someone who assisted the IRA but was not a full member.

I worked with many foreign journalists, probably because I was the one Jim could most easily spare to show them around, and probably also because I could take them into republican areas more confidently than any of the others could. Not all these foreign journalists were impressive professionals on high salaries and with lavish expense accounts. Some were young adventurers, travelling on a small budget, maybe sleeping in a motor caravan. They were just travellers who hoped they could mine a bit of money for themselves out of the trouble in Northern Ireland. Marc, the man from *Ebony*, was the one who intrigued me most.

Marc Crawford — or Marwil Cooper Crawford — had been a friend of Stephen's a year before in Mexico. He had had deep experience of both war and inter-communal strife, before he came to Belfast. He had been a master sergeant in the US army during the war in Korea and, as a reporter covering the integration of Central High School in Little Rock, Arkansas, he was kicked in the teeth then arrested and jailed for biting his attacker's foot. So he was well prepared by experience to understand Northern Ireland. He had even been a PR man for BB King. Now he taught creative writing and jazz appreciation, and he was a strong counter to Jim's insistence that journalism wasn't for people who wanted to be writers.

Marc was approaching the end of his stay and was losing his ebullience. He had seen enough to know that Northern Ireland's trouble was no joke.

'Where is your friend, the fog inspector?' asked the barman in the Duke of York one day.

'He'll be in later.'

Marc greeted all the stares, of those not used to seeing black people, with a wide playful smile, which blew away any fear of him. He was loud and brash. This, I suppose, was the work he had to do, to be accepted. Not that I considered that at the time, but I have seen other self-conscious black men employ the same device and relax into being serious and thoughtful when they were freed of the burden of being a novelty. So my impression of him at first was that he was hugely sociable but superficial. Then he put the work into learning about Belfast and, in the end, he was saddened by the discovery that this division was deep and that the trouble was likely to go on for a long time. He was sure about that before he left.

We drank together in Kelly's. We walked the length of North Street the day it was bombed and every window was broken. I talked to him about the near impossibility of getting a girlfriend in Belfast at that time. However, one possible source of sexual opportunity, I began to think, might be this very stream of foreign journalists. One of the journalists I guided was an American photographer called Aileen. Aileen was a large bulky woman who drank with the men and worked on rough stories. She was a photographer and used a little Leica which was plastered with black insulating tape — though whether to hold it together or to improve her grip, or just to make it look more workmanlike, I don't know.

Aileen was fascinated by the challenge of photographing petrol bombs and burning buildings at night. Later, another photographer published an article recommending the f-stop and shutter-speed combinations for a range of riot situations. Someone taught Aileen to enhance exposure by prolonging the developing period and she was excited about that. I took her to the Markets and around the Falls but didn't go out to riots with her. One evening, walking back to

Kelly's, I turned and chanced a kiss.

'God, you act like you haven't had it for six months,' she said.

I was thinking that once in six months would be good.

Okay, she would take me back to her hostel. We walked hand-in-hand through the streets. I was embarrassed to be with such an unattractive woman, however generous she was. She was perhaps twice my bulk but then who was doing whom a favour here? We met Martin Rosatto and I cringed at the thought of him relaying what he had seen to the crowd in Kelly's. Then again, maybe he was impressed.

Aileen was staying in a hostel near the City Hall. She went up first to check that no one on the staff would see her taking me to her room. I waited. She came down and said that a warden was about, but I should come in and sit with her until his back was turned. The reception area on the first floor was just a bare clinical room with few adornments. Formica-topped tables and ashtrays. It was designed to reject flicks and spills and to be easily cleaned. We sat and waited for the man in the brown jacket to disappear. I felt nervous and apprehensive and, I suppose, cheap. I had no actual affection for Aileen.

'You're a funny wee man,' she said, stroking my head.

'Hey, we'll have none of that in here,' barked the warden, who had clearly been waiting for his suspicion to be confirmed.

'This isn't going to work,' I said.

'We could go to a hotel.'

'Naw, let's leave it....'

Marc said he thought that the paucity of sexual opportunity in a war zone would make a great story. Who better to interview about it than myself? On the day he left, he came into the office with a tape recorder and, in front of Jim and

Paddy and the others, he said: 'Malachi, I want to record an interview with you about how you can't get laid.'

'No chance.'

'It's no trouble, man. Come on, give me ten minutes. It's a great story. It's the kind of insight you don't get from anywhere else. Come on now.'

I was embarrassed and tried to make light of my refusal.

Jim said: 'Go and give him a couple of quotes about how you can't get a girl, Malachi. What's wrong that you can't oblige the guy?'

Paddy said: 'You'll be famous in America. They'll all be sympathising with how you can't get a woman.'

Rick and Eddie were grinning.

'Who says I can't get a woman?'

'You did,' said Jim.

'Och, leave the wee lad alone,' said Paddy.

'No interview?' said Mark.

'I'll write something and send it to you,' I promised.

I never did.

# Part Six

# Chapter 28

The columnist Observer could have been writing to me personally after Bloody Friday:

> Can anyone with a shred of decency any longer support or condone, even accept in silence, such acts of brutal and calculated murder? I address the question especially to those people in areas where these enemies of society seek sanctuary, plan their vile deeds and store the implements of death and destruction. Those people of the Falls, Andersonstown, Ballymurphy and the Bogside, who profess to be Christian, must take whatever steps are humanly possible to dissociate themselves from the men of violence.

But how? I could see the boys of the IRA pass my living-room window with their guns, presumably going to a dump just yards away. I could hardly have exposed them more than they were already exposing themselves. And I had little faith that if I did bring the police and army into the area to raid safe houses and dumps, they would not have arrested or even killed innocents at the same time. But I also felt that my life in the middle of all this was untenable.

The danger in Belfast made it difficult for me to contemplate moving out of the family home, to another part of the city. I would have felt like I was deserting my family and affronting my mother. Stephen said: 'In Canada, it's no big deal to move out from your parents' and take an apartment.'

Here it was.

'But you would be better getting out to fuck altogether.' He was already thinking about his own escape, putting a date on it: April, or perhaps just after Christmas. And I wouldn't have wanted to stay on at *The Sunday News* after Stephen was gone anyway.

'I'm going,' I yelled at Barney one night. 'I'm going to Canada.'

'Go. Thank God Ireland has some men with the courage to stay and serve their country, but my son hasn't.'

'That's ridiculous. It is those men who are making a mess of this place.'

'Sometimes history delivers a challenge,' he said, as if quoting someone. 'And some men can meet it and some can run.'

We should have had the sense not even to talk about it. The news would come on. The IRA had killed someone. I'd scowl at him: 'Where was the sense in that?'

'Don't talk when you don't know. There'd have been a reason for that.'

Observer was, at least, acquiring a realistic sense of how long the troubles were likely to go on. Reflecting on the murder of baby Alan Jack, cut to shreds by flying glass from a bomb, he wrote: 'Just think of the chat in some "patriot's" home in 15 or 20 years hence. "What did you do for the cause, Da?" — "I planted a bomb that blew a child into eternity".'

What I was wrestling with was the same as what Observer was wrestling with — the failure of moral judgment to make any change to what people were doing. We know now that people who killed babies rationalised what they did and are spoken of as valued leaders of their communities; that political parties and even government ministers have pleaded for compassion for, and indulgence of, those who have blown up babies; that there would be no peace without the concession that the bomber of babies had a point. The bomber of babies also benefits from a Christian presumption of redemption, years after the deed, though no Christian presumptions hindered him at the time. Indeed, usually he isn't asking for redemption even now.

A week later, the invasion of the no-go areas was accurately predicted on our front page. Four thousand new troops came in to prepare for it. It would begin the next day.

On that Saturday night, I went out with one of the photographers on a story. We were walking up Donegall Street when an army pig crashed through the lights from the other side, hit a car on Royal Avenue and, in trying to recover, ploughed into a line of cars that had stopped at traffic lights on our side. Bob, the photographer, started taking pictures while I went from car to car, to see if I could help the injured. A man sat stunned at his steering wheel, with blood pouring from a forehead wound. He had no idea what had happened.

The pig had been carrying a wounded soldier. He had shot himself by accident.

This made a dramatic photo feature for the front page. I was impressed that Bob's need for pictures overrode any urge to help the injured. There would be others to do that, but only one person with a camera. One of his pictures shows a man standing beside the wrecked cars, reading a newspaper, as if he hasn't even noticed what has happened.

When I walked back into the office with blood on my shirt, Stephen thought, at first, that I had been attacked.

Our headline was strangely muted: 'Tale of an Accident'. Nowadays it would be more scathing: *Jinxed Army Unit's Double Cock-up*

*'First a squaddie shoots himself and then the vehicle rushing*

*him to hospital crashes into a line of parked cars at traffic lights. And these men are in the front line against the* IRA. *God help us all.'*

I presume a policy of not embarrassing the army determined that the story should carry no implied criticism. It was probably a similar policy that had spiked my story about the killings in Springhill. This same issue carried a full-page ad from Corry's woodyard, to refute the speculation about the yard having been used as a sniping position.

The IRA had tried to burn down Corry's and claimed this as a response to requests made by local residents. The advertisement explained the yard owner's take on events.

> We have enjoyed good relations with responsible members of our neighbouring Catholic community, and we have given considerable financial and material assistance to (amongst others) the Westrock Tenants Association and the Springhill Catholic Ex-Servicemen's Association. A community centre in Westrock, to which we gave £250, was engulfed by the fire.
>
> The fire also destroyed some of the Catholic bungalows in Westrock. This was due to the intense heat and flying sparks. These homes would have been saved if two fire engines, which were sent to deal with the bungalow fires, had not been prevented from getting there by the IRA who hijacked them and threatened the lives of the crews until all appliances and men were withdrawn from our timber yard.

The IRA had clearly been determined that Corry's timber yard would be destroyed. The Provisionals' case was that snipers had used the yard, on the day the ceasefire ended, as a base from which to kill innocent civilians.

> There have been NO 'hooded or masked gunmen' shooting from our timber yard into the Catholic estates (the presence of our maintenance men, who wear masks when cleaning the boilers, may have given rise to this allegation).

> The army (who requisitioned areas of our yard, and built an observation post) have fired at identified gunmen from our timber yard.

However, it was not 'identified gunmen' who had been killed on 9 July.

Rather than air both sides of this dispute, *The Sunday News* had gone for the advertiser's money, and the advertiser had bought space to defend not only the reputation of Corry's but the reputation of the army too, even to the point of alleging, in effect, that innocent people who had been shot by soldiers firing from Corry's timber yard had been armed.

Was it J.P. Corry's job to adjudicate on that? Any more than it was the job of the Ulster Unionist Party to determine that Catholics who had been found lying on waste ground with bullets in their heads were members of the IRA?

No one said to my face that I should be doing more to help the army against the IRA but they all knew that I was living closer to the IRA than they were. Little sense of my proximity to that organisation comes out of my journalism of that time, but people may have wondered about the detail in my minefield story about the explosives expert, 'not from the area'. Who was I to be harbouring secrets about bomb-makers and their movements, only to be hinting at them in stories for the paper? My reserve about these things was defensible in terms of the need to keep journalism separate from policing. That, in itself, was a tenuous argument when the bombs threatened the city you worked in and the people with whom you worked.

I could have pleaded the need to defend sources if I had been producing valuable stories with real insights that might inform society about the problem of political violence. Very little of what I did had value in those terms. This was excusable in a beginner living in fear, but left me with no right to claim that I was an investigator who needed the freedom to keep secrets from the state about the IRA bombers trying to bring that state down.

My own defence, if someone had said to me that I should be trying to garner information for the police about the IRA, would have been more like this: I would be killed by the IRA if they thought I was doing that; my family would be driven from their home and innocent people would be endangered. How good was the state's record of saving lives? And, anyway, the men I directed them to would be interned, which was unjust. And besides, the army must know where these men were without my having to tell them.

Those in army vehicles passing up Finaghy Road North along the motorway past Riverdale knew what direction the shots were coming from; they were constantly raiding houses around me, and it was plain to me that many of the people being taken away were not IRA men at all but often people who had been minding a rifle for someone — perhaps under duress — or perhaps, for all I knew, had had evidence planted on them.

I was getting drunk and maudlin too often. I would lapse into self-pity and a self-aggrandising whine to solicit sympathy for the horrors I was bravely enduring, so close to the dangerous action. My moans and boasts were often dangerously candid, and if the men of E Company had known how freely I discussed their movements, they would have seen me as a danger to them. I knew that. I also knew that I was simply too immature to survive between the secrecy the street demanded and the carnival of storytelling that was my other life.

Soon Paddy and Stephen knew that I had knowledge of the kind the police wanted and it shocked me that they thought I should go to the police and tell them where I had seen men go for guns. 'If there is a dump there, they just go in and get the stuff. What's so hard about that? Why would anyone know it was anything to do with you?'

I didn't consider then that by talking about this I was

putting them in fear of dangerous responsibilities too. One day in the bar, I talked about E Company and said: 'I know where their guns are. I watch them going back and forth across the gardens in our street. It's under my nose.'

Poor Stephen sneaked away and called the police and then panicked and hung up, agonising in the same way as I did about whether or not to take the responsibility of interfering. All my reasoning pared my resolve back to one simple fact: I was scared they would kill me if I exposed them! I was scared they were already wondering if I was a risk, and I was a risk.

But I would soon get a clear invitation to tell what I knew.

One day, Jim announced: 'The police are offering us a visit to their museum in Enniskillen.'

I was to call the press officer and arrange to go in his car. This had not happened before.

'Why don't I go in the photographer's car?'

'They're going to provide the photographs themselves.'

I phoned a man whom I will call 'Norman'.

'I'll pick you up at your house in the morning.'

'God, no. I'll come to yours.'

'We'll meet in between.'

So he didn't want me to know where he lived. He had to take care against the IRA finding that out from me. The next morning, I stood on a street corner on the Antrim Road and his maroon car pulled up.

'Malachi?'

'Yes.'

'Get in.'

Had this assignment been set up by the police, to give them a chance to speak to me, and see if I could be recruited as an informant? That was my fear. He was not warm; he was barely civil, which makes me doubt on reflection that he was there to manipulate me. A charmer would have nudged me over a line to disclosing valuable details without my even noticing what he had done. Maybe the RUC, in those days, didn't have any charmers.

We drove west along the motorway, past Riverdale and the nest of snipers who were probably all still asleep, out into open countryside, past the Long Kesh internment camp, towards the more meandering roads of Tyrone and Fermanagh. Norman asked me about my ambitions. I told him that I wanted to progress in journalism, that I had thought of emigrating to Canada. We didn't discuss politics or policing at first. He must have thought me a strangely incurious journalist. I did say I didn't think that I could go on living in Northern Ireland.

'I'd have thought this was a very good place for a journalist to be?'

'Maybe I'm too close to it.'

'You're afraid you can't be objective about it?'

'I'm not sure that Fleet Street wants objectivity anyway. But they do want to keep it simple, and it isn't simple, is it?'

'Armed men want to overthrow the state against the democratically expressed wishes of the people? Seems simple enough to me.'

'Different people have different ideas of what the state is, or should be.'

'If they don't like it, they are free to change it, so long as they use the democratic system.'

'They are not going to get the democratic chance to remove the border — that one is loaded against them. It was drawn to enclose a majority in favour of it.'

Now we were taking sides against each other on the old central question which we should have had the sense to avoid. I was talking like a taig and he was talking like a prod. Neither of us was giving credit to the other's basic position or even trying to see the other's point of view. 'Don't you realise that the Protestants of Ulster are not going to budge while there is a gun at their heads?'

'They aren't the only ones with a gun at their heads. I am

as much in danger of the British army as I am of the IRA.'

'That's ridiculous.'

'Not to me, it's not.'

'Well, the IRA could get rid of the army in the morning simply by putting down their guns.'

'I wish they would.'

'Really? You were beginning to sound like one of them for a minute.'

'That's what worries me — that so many people can't tell the difference.'

Did he know how he sounded to me? Like someone impervious to questions about his own politics. What if I told him that the reason people bombed Belfast was that they were sick of trying to reason with smug and righteous Protestant men who thought the bottom line was always and only law and order and the status quo? Did he not know that this line of reasoning and this patrician manner, when voiced by unionist politicians, in their efforts to dissuade the Catholic community from supporting the IRA, only made things worse?

'I think you should see how the violence evolved out of bad politics. We wouldn't have got to this if the Civil Rights campaign had been listened to,' I said.

'Do you really believe that? What rights do you think the people who bombed the Abercorn were looking for? The IRA is building its own power base to assert its own demands. It's not representing you.'

Once into Tyrone, out from under the shadow of Belfast, it was easier to relax and talk more personally or even to sit silently for miles and leave the talking to Norman.

'I think that the only responsible position anyone can take is to support the state against the terrorists and leave it to the democratic system itself to resolve our problems. I might want Ulster to be British; you might want it to be Irish. No one in their right mind wants it to be torn apart. And what freedoms do you think the IRA will allow you if they take over?'

'They are not going to take over,' I said.

Which left us silent for a few miles.

'If I was a young man living in Andersonstown, with the IRA all around me, I would tell the police everything I knew.'

'Do you think many people do that?' I said.

'There is a reward for information but you never hear any stories about it being paid out. Doesn't mean that it hasn't been. And it could take a young man like you a long way, to a new life.'

Now all I had to do, I assumed, was say, 'Yes, okay; here's the address of the safe house; here's roughly where the arms dump is.' And I was petrified by how easy it would have been, like stepping off a cliff.

I said nothing, because my whole life would have changed in a moment if I had. I would have had responsibility, too, for actions that would have changed the lives of others as radically. And Norman did not press me any further. The police may have been more interested in an informant who would continue to live in Riverdale — a man who was as eager as I was now to leave was no use to them.

The story I wrote about the museum we visited exudes an enthusiasm that contrasts with the sour mood of the day in the car. You would think to read it that I had had a fun day out. I described the museum as a criminal's paradise, with loaded dice, forged currency and burglary tools.

> A display piece shows the history of sectarian rioting and IRA campaigns through the ages and no matter how far back you go the familiar names are there: York Street, Carrick Hill, Falls Road and Short Strand. The pattern is still the same.

Did that not make Norman wonder if there was something fundamentally wrong that fired people up in every generation?

# Chapter 29

One Sunday night in late July, I went with Fegan and Maguire to the club in the Markets, the one in the tannery that had been 'liberated' by the Official IRA, where every singsong included 'The Ballad of Joe McCann'. We liked to go to other bars too, but many of these were now turning away strangers at the door. The club in Lagan Street was cheap and lively. A man I didn't know passed me with a warm smile and a hand on the shoulder.

'How do you know him?' Maguire asked.

'I don't.' I presumed he was one of the masked gunmen I had seen on the Land-Rover patrol. Tommy Conlon was there and checked that we were enjoying ourselves but later he come over and took me outside. 'It's best you go home. Whitelaw is going to move into the no-go areas and take down the barricades tonight. If you don't leave now, you mightn't get out of the area.' Tommy sounded as if he expected serious fighting.

Fegan and Maguire were impressed by the news. 'But how would the Stickies know about this?'

'Whitelaw has just announced it on television.'

We left. Back in Riverdale, the barricades were still up.

Maguire dropped me off on the main Finaghy Road and I walked into the estate. I passed the vigilantes at the barricade. What were they expecting to do — fend off a huge invasion by the British army? Surely not.

At eight, my mother woke me. 'There's a soldier on the doorstep.' I looked out and there were army vehicles in the street and armed soldiers on the corners.

'No riot?'

The IRA hadn't resisted the invasion. The most sensible thing they had done in their campaign so far was to retreat in the face of overwhelming force. The news said that three car-bombs had shattered Claudy and killed several people, including small children. What was the sense in that? I couldn't see any at all, unless it was just a kick to show that the IRA was still alive. The bombers had given no warning. It later came out that the telephones in the area had not been working because the IRA had previously bombed a local exchange. The bomb team had tried to phone a warning through and had scoured the area for a phone that worked. It was their own fault that none did. At first, however, the IRA denied responsibility. Seán MacStíofáin even claimed later to have conducted an investigation and confirmed that none of his units had been responsible. He was lying.

Claudy is a small town in the Sperrin mountains, by the main road to Derry. The bombings there spawned a song, by James Simmons — one of the best anti-war songs I have heard: 'And Christ, little Catherine Eaken is dead.'

It is hard to think of any tactical value to the bombing of Claudy that warranted the risk that civilians might die. There were no significant commercial targets in this small mountain village. The IRA logic for bombing, say the Abercorn in Belfast, was that it could disrupt the commercial life of the city. This would damage the British Exchequer and stand as a colossal act of armed propaganda. What sense was there in disrupting the commercial life of a village?

The bombs may have been intended to stretch forces away from the invasion of the Bogside and the Creggan. This presupposes that the IRA had planned to resist the army. It had, in fact, chosen to melt away. And if the aim was to stretch the army, hoax bombs would have done as well. They would have tied down soldiers in evacuating and sealing the village for the hours it would have taken to check that the bombs were not real. Detonating real bombs tied down ambulances and medical services that the IRA itself would have needed, had the invasion of the no-go areas turned bloody.

It made no sense at all to bomb Claudy.

And it is also likely that the bombs had been made ready before Whitelaw had announced that he was taking down the barricades. The attack was pointless and incompetent. It succeeded in only one thing: killing a near equal number of Catholics and Protestants, and of pensioners and children. But long before this, the IRA must have decided that if killing civilians wasn't actually a desirable outcome, the risk of it was to be no deterrent to an attack plan. It was better to let the attack go ahead because the satisfaction of bombing a town would never be outweighed by the shame of having killed innocents.

Perhaps, in the IRA's way of seeing things, there were no innocents.

Thirty years later, the police disclosed that the main suspect had been a Catholic priest. They didn't name him, but the press took this to be a reference to Fr James Chesney, who had been named in an anonymous letter to the Mayor of Derry. Chesney was dead. The Church by then had suspected he was a dangerous republican activist and had shifted him to a remote parish in Donegal, there to go on hearing the confessions of lesser sinners than himself. Northern Ireland Office documents revealed that the case of

Fr Chesney had been discussed by William Whitelaw and the Primate of Ireland, Cardinal Conway, in December 1972. Whitelaw had expressed his disgust at the behaviour of the bomber priest. Still, Chesney was not arrested but transferred to a parish over the border in Raphoe, and later farther north to Malin.

One can only speculate on why the British did not arrest Chesney; had a priest been charged with leading an IRA bomb team, that might too easily have confirmed the loyalist prejudice that the IRA and the Catholic Church were close allies, and prompted loyalist paramilitaries to target all priests. The government had the power to intern him, but this would have roused considerable wrath and fear among Catholics, and would have seemed to confirm to them that the state was anti-Catholic. There were no gains for the state in moving against him. An undercover squad might have been sent to assassinate him but that would have stoked up sectarian violence.

The army now surrounded Andersonstown and built several new barracks compounds. They took over the Gaelic football ground at Casement Park; they reinforced Andersonstown police station; they built a new camp at the top of Slievegallion Drive; they extended and buttressed their base in Lenadoon. Andersonstown was surrounded and the army was on the inside, and could no longer be barricaded out.

Jim arranged for me to go around all the bases with a photographer, to take pictures of them and mark them on a map of the area. He hired a photographer who usually worked for the *Sunday Independent*. Our own photographers were afraid to go into the area. Patrick was a light-hearted and friendly man who enjoyed his work. Not being part of the culture of *The Sunday News*, he had no sense of my being the office junior who was to be patronised. We were simply professionals doing a job together without any presumption at work that one was senior to the other. Some journalists, for some reason, sneer at every story they work on, probably because, after a time, nothing is new to them. Patrick wasn't like that.

We went first to the graveyard opposite Andersonstown police station and moved around the plots, trying to find a good angle to foreground an impressive headstone. 'That's where I started school in Belfast,' I told him when we reached Casement Park. The parish school had not been built yet and the priest had put us in the smelly pavilion. The tang of wet concrete and sweat is one I can still recall with ease.

The base on Slievegallion Drive had been built on open common, grassy space we had played on as children. The army had built a huge corrugated-metal-sheeting wall. 'We call it Silver City,' said one of the soldiers. I wrote down 'Silver City' and used that name in the article, and Silver City is what the base came to be known as locally.

On Monagh Road, the soldiers had posted a small sign on the coils of barbed wire around them: Shooting Rights Reserved.

At Lenadoon, a soldier came out, crouched on one knee and pointed his rifle at Patrick. An officer stepped out and signalled me to approach him.

'What are you doing?' He was Asian.

We showed him our press cards. The officer radioed to all units that there were a couple of 'spooks' in the area. That was us. My understanding was that we did not need army permission to photograph public places, but I rationalised it as an acceptable courtesy to inform them of what we were doing. Jim, back at the office, did his favourite Sandhurst impersonation of the call he had taken from the army press office: 'I say, one of your chaps is making a fucking nuisance of himself up in Andahsunstan.'

A lot of work went into laying out the map and pictures, but it ended up as half a page above a half-page advertisement.

'Sorry,' said Jim. 'Kind of kills it.'

Sometimes it wasn't possible to be a journalist watching the trouble as from the outside. One Saturday morning, I was at the front of the house with my sister Bríd when a commotion broke out. Three men came charging across our neighbour's garden and over the hedge into ours, then right in front of us up the path to the street. Straight after them on foot came a group of British soldiers with their rifles. I had understood that if you ran from the army you were in danger of being shot. These men must have had reason to think it was worth the risk.

Some of the soldiers chased the men up the street and caught them, while one stood guard on our path and others brought around the red car the men had leapt from. I walked up to the soldier in the path and showed him my press card. 'Can you tell me what is happening here?'

'No.'

Bríd hissed at me, 'Are you out of your head?'

I wasn't sure myself whether I was doing my job or showing off.

'I am a journalist. I have to find out what's going on.'

'You're a bloody eejit.'

We stood in the street and watched the soldiers take the men into a personnel carrier. One of them followed, driving the red car. That night, at work, I called the army press office. I said: 'I witnessed an event today in which three men in a red car were arrested in Riverdale. Could you give me some background on that?'

'I have no information on that.'

'Well I saw it happen.' I gave him the time and the location.

'I'll get back to you.' An hour later, the press officer called back and dictated the details of five separate incidents in which three men had been detained after a red car, acting suspiciously, had been intercepted by soldiers. None was the incident I had seen.

'You're trying to confuse me, aren't you?'

'This is the only answer I have to your question.'

On a Sunday afternoon, I went out to watch a massive riot on the Andersonstown Road, organised to protest against the occupation of Casement Park, the Gaelic sports ground. Some men had got hold of a huge telegraph pole, to use it as a battering ram against the gates. They made a good picture for the next day's papers but God knows what they thought they were going to do if they succeeded in breaking through the gates: fight the army hand-to-hand? The soldiers would have had to shoot them.

The army held a line across the road and took a pelting of rocks on their shields but there were hundreds, perhaps thousands, of men on the road and, if they had all surged forward, they would have been similarly more powerful than was safe for them. Then suddenly, the army charged.

I fell back about one hundred yards, like most people, and relaxed before it dawned on me that the soldiers were still coming, that they were going to push everyone about a half-mile or more up the road. I tried to affect a lack of urgency. If I ran, I was a target because I was betraying my guilt. The challenge was to move quickly but somehow nonchalantly. If I were arrested, I could show my press card, but what if they hit me over the head first? I heard the blasts of several rubber bullets being fired into the crowd. Now everyone was running as fast as they could, and scattering into the estates to either side of us. The soldiers were within reach of me when I got to the top of Finaghy Road North. Would any of them be able to work out for themselves that the reason I wasn't still running was that I felt that I wasn't part of the riot. The whole premise that acting innocently would spare me an arrest or an injury was, of course, predicated on a gamble that these soldiers cared whether I was innocent or not.

Simon Winchester of the *Guardian* and another reporter were standing at the top of Finaghy Road North by the petrol station. Now, *they* looked like real journalists. They were in no danger. I stopped and stood near them, tried to catch Simon's eye and say hello, tried to mingle with my fellows. Did I know Simon well enough to join his company? He had been affable when we had met before. How would he take to my hiding behind him? I felt that by cowering near Simon, I was betraying a lack of confidence in my equal right to be there. I was like a child clinging to his daddy's trouser leg: See, I am a journalist too. But Simon looked like a journalist and I didn't. I looked like another man of my generation from Andersonstown. I looked like what I was.

The soldiers at the head of the charge fanned out to positions on each side of the Andersonstown Road. One of them — a large, round-faced black man — squatted in the shop doorway. He pointed his rubber-bullet gun at me. I noticed with alarm that he was conspicuously afraid. He was glancing sharply all around him to check for other threats, but returning his gaze each time, as quickly as he could, to me. He was out of breath from the run and his heavy uniform with flak jacket and equipment must have been horribly uncomfortable. He was hardly poised to fight. And he was afraid of me. I might have a pistol or a blast bomb behind my back. I might even just rush forward and kick him in the face and grab his gun. I hadn't the least notion of doing that, but how was he to know? The other soldiers supporting this man were still farther back down the road. He was exposed. If the IRA had posted snipers, say, in the church grounds behind me, in anticipation of this charge, he was a clear target and he knew it. If they hadn't posted snipers there, why not? It seemed the obvious thing to do.

I raised my hands and tried to move aside from the line of his aim. His aim followed me. What was I to do — shrug benignly, show a little perplexity and hope that it would pass for innocence? I took out my press card and held it up. He still kept his fearful aim directly fixed on me. I turned and walked briskly away, hoping the frightened soldier would not fire. He didn't.

On 6 August, the paper led with the story of the wedding of one of the women injured in the bomb at the Abercorn. Rosaleen McNern had lost both her legs and her right arm and an eye. At the ceremony in Killybegs, Rosaleen's chief bridesmaids were her sisters, Bernadette and Jennifer. Jennifer was also in a wheelchair, having lost both legs in the same explosion. Rosaleen said: 'I am very happy and bear no resentment against anybody for my injuries.'

Sometimes it was plain that those who delivered IRA bombs were inept and ill-equipped rather than callous.

The IRA bomb-makers devised an anti-handling device for bombs. These bombs had no timers but were triggered by the efforts of army bomb-disposal experts to disarm them. This was a way of preventing civilian deaths. The area could be cleared in time and reporters and others could gather at a safe distance to watch the explosion. Then, as the competition with the army experts increased, the IRA countered with an ordinary timer-controlled bomb, nailed into its casing to disguise it as a bomb with an anti-handling device. The trouble with these bombs, for the teams delivering them, was that they could not disarm them.

One bomber told me that he had been 'crapping himself' when delivering one of the first of these and realised the weakness in it.

In August, two young people, 18-year-old Anne Parker from Ballymurphy, a member of Cumann na mBan, and 23-year-old Michael Clarke, a Provo, died when they tried to abort an attack on a store in North Howard Street, between the Shankill and the Falls. The IRA's own tribute to them in *Tírghrá* says that they were forced to cancel the attack because there were civilians in the area. Maybe now, after Bloody Friday, the IRA was more sensitive to the danger of killing civilians. The bomb exploded in their car as Parker and Clarke returned 'to base'. It seems they had had no means available to them of disarming it. Whatever went wrong, there would still be an explosion, somewhere. It appears to have been more important, to those who sent them, that a bomb would go off somewhere, than that the people delivering it would return alive. How callous is that?

The paper was, as ever, concerned with the sexual behaviour of the population, and reported the increase in young women travelling to England for abortions. This was accompanied by a rise in what was then called VD — venereal disease. The country's leading consultant venereologist declared himself alarmed at the incidence of infection among girls as young as 14, but 'wasn't aware of recent reports that there had been a rash of tropical conditions introduced into the city by journalists coming here to cover the troubles direct from Vietnam and other Asian countries.'

So presumably there was no truth in those reports and, therefore, no need to mention them in the story.

Abby continued to dispense her callous advice to the insecure:

> Last year my skin fell into wrinkles around my eyes and I became so embarrassed I stopped going out with my husband because he made remarks.
>
> Depressed

> Dear Depressed, I feel it would be wise for you to seek psychiatric counselling. PS ask your doctor to recommend a plastic surgeon.

I had my first flight and my first trip to England that month. I'd heard about two Belfast men who had sailed across the Atlantic in a 30-foot yacht. Someone told me afterwards that this was no great achievement but I think it made a good travel piece anyway. Jim suggested I ask Pat to send me to the Isle of Wight to interview them. Pat said yes and I flew out on a British Caledonian flight to London, with Cecil, the chief photographer on the paper. Our photographers might have been unwilling to accompany me into Riverdale, but they were happy to go to the Isle of Wight.

Noticing that I was wincing at the accents of the porters in Victoria Station, Cecil said, 'They're not soldiers. Get used to it.'

Our story nearly fell through because only one of the brothers was at home. Joe McKitterick told us nothing he couldn't have told me on the phone but he showed us the boat and dug out a picture of his brother Jack on the yacht with the skyline of Manhattan behind him.

Instead of squandering our expense account on a hotel room, Cecil suggested we just walk around London for a few hours and then take a bench at Victoria Station. He showed me Soho and the prostitutes but we didn't trade. We walked past black rubbish bags left out on the street, which we would have been wary of in Belfast, but the big impression here was of a city that was free and alive and busy. It must already have occurred to the IRA how easy it would be to strike here. The following year, they did.

# Chapter 30

Everyone was awake when I got home from my holiday in August. Maguire and I had hitchhiked to Amsterdam. The police at Heysham had searched me thoroughly. 'No guns,' I joked. They'd been looking not for guns but for drugs. They *should* have been looking for guns. It was all the police and army on the other side of the Irish Sea had time to think about. The army had just searched our house. My mother was excited. It was something to talk about and it was better not to be spared when every other house was getting searched. What would the neighbours think? Mum said: 'One thing's clear; they know everything. They know all the safe houses and all the names. They know everything.'

That was a relief.

Two weeks after Operation Motorman and the dismantling of the barricades, the paper reported that the army believed that the IRA was still as dangerous as it had been before the opening up of the no-go areas. On 13 August, we reported that — aside from the arrest of Martin Meehan, the officer commanding the third battalion, which included Ardoyne — the command structure of the Provisional IRA was thought to be the same as before. Seamus Twomey, the

Belfast Brigade leader, was hiding, but other prominent Republicans had been seen walking openly in Andersonstown. The leader of the Provisionals in Derry, Martin McGuinness, was said to have come back from Buncrana and to be 'on duty' in the Creggan area. While away, he had been married by Fr Denis Bradley. Moreover, both wings of the IRA were better armed, if this could be judged from the type of weapons being captured by the British army.

Then, on 3 September, the paper led with a report of a deepening split within the Provisionals and a failed plot to assassinate the Chief of Staff, Seán MacStíofáin. The front-page story said that the Provisionals had been left 'fragmented and bitter' by internal dissent.

> The shock defection of Maria McGuire, the IRA girl who was hunted across Europe with Provisional leader David McConnell [*sic*] after they were involved in an arms smuggling attempt in Holland, has confirmed growing suspicion in political circles in Dublin that the movement was being torn apart by internal power struggles and personality feuds.

Clearly someone on *The Sunday News* was susceptible to over-eager briefings from Dublin about splits within the IRA. But then, McGuire herself was reading too much into tensions she had observed. It is clear from her memoir that she hadn't realised how little she knew. For instance, when Ó Conaill travelled to Donegal to meet Woodfield, he simply told her that he was going to visit 'Deirdre' who was unwell.

Seamus Twomey, according to the story, had been replaced by a younger, more politically minded Belfast republican, Gerry Adams, 'a former officer commanding the Provisional unit in Ballymurphy ..., said to have much popular support within the movement'.

There was a story on 10 September about an attack on Senator Paddy Wilson. Paddy drank occasionally with Jim and me in Kelly's. He was ambushed by a group of women inside Belfast City Hall, on his way to a meeting of Belfast Corporation. 'Three women tore at Councillor Wilson's clothes as he walked through the building and he had to run to escape from them.'

The SDLP protested to the police that Councillor Lindsay Mason, another old contact of mine, was attracting a rabble to the City Hall with his protest meetings. Six months later, Paddy would be dead. He and his companion, Irene Andrews were stabbed by UDA men. One of the killers, John White, was eventually to make his way to 10 Downing Street as part of a loyalist negotiation team.

Though many horrors such as the stabbing of Paddy Wilson were to follow, in the next 30 years, the level of killing in Belfast would never again reach where it was in the summer of 1972. We thought then that it was getting worse. Stephen was resisting pressure from his father to return home to Canada. On 10 September, *The Sunday News* carried his interview with Jean Moore, the chair of the women's branch of the Loyalist Association of Workers. It gives an insight into how people saw the trouble of that period developing. Jean was campaigning for the return of Stormont, without proportional representation in the voting system. 'I was born and raised here in Crimea Street. I love every brick and paving stone and I was quite content with Ulster the way it was.' Jean saw her job with LAW and Vanguard as preparing for civil war, which she regarded as 'an almost inevitable climax to the current terror campaign'. She said: 'One of the things we are doing is to help as many of our women to learn to drive for we will need as many drivers as possible in the case of civil war.'

Stephen paraphrased her: 'of course if civil war broke out it would not mean everybody racing to the front line. Some people had to stay behind and organise evacuation to safe areas and relief centres where children and old people could go.'

People like Jean and the writers of *The Unionist Review* had not yet noticed that the loyalists were already engaged. Only in 1974 would loyalists ever again kill as many people in one year. And there would be no front line, of course. It wasn't that kind of war.

Someone else who anticipated worse was John Taylor MP, now recovering from his bullet wounds after an attempt on his life by the Official IRA. In the 24 September issue, we quoted Mr Taylor's address to a Vanguard rally in Cookstown, in which he warned Westminster that 'the people of Northern Ireland [presumably he didn't include Catholics in that category] would rise up, even in the face of the might of Britain, if they were pushed too far.'

Mr Taylor said that there would be no political solution in Northern Ireland until the IRA was defeated. If Westminster failed in its responsibility to defeat the IRA, 'then the loyalists of Ulster would have a moral responsibility to take action on their own behalf to defeat the terrorists in their midst.'

My friend Maguire had a job that summer in a lemonade factory in East Belfast, with his brother Terence, and both started going out with girls they worked with. The loyalist assassinations continued and they were both in danger. Any Catholic in a Protestant area was in danger.

I was in the office on a Saturday afternoon. Jim and Rick were making calls. 'I have a name for the guy killed on the Newtownards Road,' said Rick. 'Terence Maguire.'

'Oh fuck. I know him. Are you sure?'

'That's the name from the police press office.'

The Maguire I hung out with was Dennis.

'There is no danger it could have been Dennis?'

'No.' Rick had a little supercilious way with him

sometimes, to let me know he was indulging my frantic manner and would not take much more of it. I called the police and asked them to confirm the name and address. The press officer might have been giving me a weather report. We talked about deaths as if they were all stories that we handled only professionally. But he, as a policeman, must have been touched personally by some of them too. Now that the police had released the name, it would be announced on the evening news. The next of kin had been notified, but what of Maguire? I told Jim I would have to go and look for him to try to tell him before he heard it on the car radio.

'Another poor fucker plugged in a back alley,' said a reporter.

There was a strangely awkward divide now between professional and personal interests. Among the reporters there were different stock responses from those we would expect from friends. Jim, Stephen and the others were concerned for me, of course, and helpful. Stephen drove me around all the places where I thought we might find Maguire. We went to Kelly's Cellars where, again, I was strangely surrounded by attentive people, responding to my fretfulness or perhaps eager for the great social currency that a story is. And then I realised how stupid I had been to tell people in a pub that Maguire's brother had been shot. If he came in now, not knowing, there would immediately be a dozen half-drunk people around him, wanting to be the first with the news.

Back at the office, Maguire phoned me. He had heard it on the radio. He was coping by focusing on the details too. 'Are you writing the story?' I wasn't. I had simply forgotten.

'Fuck,' said Jim. 'What were you thinking of?'

I had forgotten that I was a reporter.

Stephen went out to cover another shooting that night. The name of one of the victims was Terence Martin McLaughlin. I should have recognised the name as that of my neighbour Martin, the one who had witnessed the shooting of Frank McGuinness, but I probably couldn't have coped with one more shooting to fret about. This shooting showed what a fluke it is whether we live or die. Martin was in an off-licence on Tate's Avenue during a robbery. Two hooded gunmen told him and two others to lie on the floor and then shot them. Martin took five bullets, as many as the other two put together, but he survived, though they died.

'I just was lying there wishing they would run out of bullets.'

For him, one of the worst parts of the experience was watching the other bodies take the crash of bullets into them. 'Horrific. Horrific.'

I called at the Maguire house for the wake. His sister, a nun, was there. The most important thing for the busy, attentive women who were preserving the sanity of the grief-stricken was, of course, that I should have a cup of tea and a sandwich. They produced tea in china cups and plates of sandwiches with industrial efficiency, as if any let-up in the smooth operation would open a gap that would admit floods of tears and horror. People take comfort in strangely meaningless lines: 'He was in the wrong place at the wrong time'; 'Nothing can touch him now.'

They grappled for sense in his death and for reassurance of some good in it.

'He suffered a great deal but he has been saved a great deal.'

'He is at peace now.'

'It's God's will. It was meant to be. Some other soul was spared that night.'

'They will meet their maker.'

I have seen since how others agonise incessantly over details. They wonder if they could have changed the course of events by small changes in their own behaviour.

'Maybe he called home and I wasn't in.'

Maguire's Protestant girlfriend, Ethel, came to the funeral.

She told us that the boss had offered to close the factory, to allow Terence's workmates to go too, but the workers had refused. Maguire and Ethel took a house in a Protestant area. I signed as guarantor for them with the rental agent. I was leaving Belfast now and this was the last act of authority of a salaried man. I would soon be on the dole in England. I was always nearly petrified sitting with them in their house, knowing that if they stayed long enough for the local loyalists to spot them, they would be shot too.

# Chapter 31

The IRA was determined to continue its war, regardless of what most Catholics wanted. They had the energy to defy the inertia of a large community which preferred peace and whose instincts knew that no victory was available by their means. Ultimately that decision belonged to an ambitious leadership and a rank-and-file which was armed and angry.

Loyalism had only half of that combination. It had the furious men and those men had guns, but it did not have a leadership that was prepared to contemplate years — decades — of war, and thousands of deaths. You could say that it didn't have a viable political project that could be advanced in that way. True. But neither had the Provisionals. The want of it didn't stop them.

The Vanguard leader, Bill Craig, and many of his supporters had threatened to usurp the government and launch a purge of the IRA, yet no order was given. The war that we were having was a sectarian exchange between paramilitaries attacking each other's neighbours. Why did Vanguard draw back? I suspect it was because the leaders were essentially weak men who hadn't the courage or focus that the leadership of the IRA had. They were political leaders out of a time that preceded all this urgency, just as our paper was from a different era. But that is a question I can ask only now after having gone back and studied the detail about that year. It was not one that engaged me remotely at the time. I hadn't noticed that Vanguard's bluff had already been called.

Even in my last days, the job got more adventurous and dangerous but not enough to reverse my decision to leave. One night, Stephen and I went into Andersonstown to try to find out about a man who had been kidnapped at gunpoint from a pub. We first looked for an IRA contact and called at the shebeen in South Link.

'Fuck off,' said the doorman when I told him what paper we were from. This was the paper which had described Patsy McVeigh as an 'IRA Catholic'.

'I'm local,' I said.

'Then you should be ashamed of yourself.'

Men followed us out to the car and stood debating what they should do about us, while we got in and drove off.

We called at the family home of the missing man, and his girlfriend came and sat in the car with us and talked frankly about rivalries among IRA men — the sort of material an eager journalist rarely had access to. Stephen sat at the wheel and took notes. I noticed men watching us. Suddenly I was aware that there was one at each corner of the car.

'We're going to have to get out of here.'

I asked the girl if she wanted to stay or come with us for safety.

'I'll be all right. You won't be if you hang about.'

She got out of the car and Stephen roared off down the street, wondering if shots would follow us.

I left Belfast in the autumn of 1972 with a sense that this war would go on a very long time and not be resolved. More, I went with a sense that I would never find my own bearings in life if I stayed in Riverdale. It amazed me that other men I had been to school with were eager to face imprisonment and the danger of death. Nothing in my life since has made me wish I had done it their way. I wonder if many of them wish they had done it mine.

I have tended to look back on my decision to leave as the right one. Every thing that followed in my life stemmed from that. But it was also the decision of a fraught and frightened young man who might instead have cut down on his drinking, held his nerve and survived. I wasn't going to change overnight on the Heysham boat into a mature adult who would know how to handle relationships, establish a calm centre in my life and earn a living. All I was escaping to was the ordinary challenges that face the young unemployed male. Better that any day, though, than the misery of a city saturated with murder, in which the only relief was the unsustainable fantasy that you understood. I left a better newspaper than the one I had joined, though it wasn't I who made it better. What made it better was the collapse of the fantasy that had sustained it, the fantasy that Northern Ireland could outstare the horror and keep its mind instead on simple homely things.

Billy the thief advised me on how to secure my right to unemployment benefit. 'If you just walk out of your job, you'll get no dole for six weeks, so you have to have a medical reason for going. You've got to get a note from your doctor saying this place has shattered your nerves.'

So I did. I told a young GP that I needed to go because I was living in constant fear of being killed. His note, which I still have, says that I was suffering from an anxiety neurosis. Was it neurotic to be afraid when danger was real? Nobody asked — not the doctor or the dole clerk in England. But had I turned up at the dole and said I had left a job because I was afraid, that in itself would not have entitled me to any money. 'Bombs and bullets' hadn't been an acceptable excuse in Belfast on internment day, and it wouldn't be here either.

From even before I left, and for years after, I agonised often about whether I had done the right thing in walking away from a salary and a career. Many of the reasons I gave myself for going turned out not to be as strong as they felt at the time. The civil war had already peaked and was finding a routine that it would maintain for decades. I was getting the hang of journalism, despite that having seemed at first unlikely. Journalism itself on that paper might not have been the best engagement with the troubles but it wasn't perfect anywhere. You can't fault *The Sunday News* in particular for not having understood the secret machinations behind the ceasefire when no one else understood them either. And I wouldn't have had to stay on *The Sunday News*, or even at home. And if the problem was that I was drinking too much and not finding a girl, I could have dealt with that as others did. Ultimately the problem was that I was too young and restless. I had the resources to manage my own life in Belfast, a salary double my father's, but I hadn't the time or the patience. My older self says to my younger one: *Stay. Your vocation is journalism and this is the story. Surely there is someone who can advise you on how to get a flat in a safe area and manage your life. There are new friends to make. Take your time. Get serious about your work.*

Tommy Gorman had found unlikely allies among the mothers of Riverdale who would give him a bed, store his bombs and raise the alarm when soldiers came into the street. He was having the time of his life, fitting in. I could have crossed the street at any time and said: 'Can I be in your gang?' Others did. But the fit was wrong. Barney had said, 'You're more concerned to make a living' — as if it were contemptible to be looking after your own needs at such a time. So I gave it away. I would have some moral advantage, then, over the man who was leaving for promotion; I was leaving for the dole.

Ultimately I was appalled that neighbours were

prolonging the war, and for some it was just to have more purpose and excitement in their lives. My older self also says to the younger one on the boat: *You still don't even know the basics of living, how to manage loneliness and live off the dole; Belfast is the wrong place to learn these things. Tommy Gorman and the boys will develop personally in the prisons — you have to find your own path, even your own prison. What do you know about how to befriend women? Nothing. You are too hungry. Go away and grow up in some place where you are less likely to get killed trying.*

The decision to go was a jump in the dark, a moment of exhilarating abandon, like blowing the whistle in the night in protest against soldiers and war, and even against silly women with bin lids. My going was a kind of mock suicidal gesture. I left Belfast drunk. The Tannoy on the ferry called my name and I hardly believed it but made my way up on deck. Below on the dock, Fegan and Stephen were waving to me and yelling. They were drunk too. I threw a leg over the barrier, affecting to be climbing off the boat. The bursar pulled me back.

'Idiot,' I thought. 'Can't he see I'm only codding?'

But I wanted to go back into the city with Fegan and Stephen, and wondered if my grand gesture of leaving Belfast and my job and my friends had already gone too far.

# Epilogue

I had one brief return to Belfast for Christmas 1972. On Christmas Eve, coming home from town in a black 'people's' taxi up the Falls Road, the woman opposite me was laughing cheerfully with her husband. I couldn't make out her face in the shadow but I recognised the voice.

'It's Máire, isn't it?'

Máire and Jimmy Drumm were in the best of form, perhaps enjoying the brief respite of a Christmas ceasefire, perhaps feeling pleased with the year behind them. It was like seeing one of your teachers on holiday and marvelling at how lightly he has put away his scowl. Maybe she assumed that if I knew her I must be one of her boys, one of her bombers. 'Have a lovely Christmas, son,' she said when I got out.

It was another seven years before I came back to Belfast again. Then Jim gave me freelance work. He said, 'The Pope is coming to Ireland and the papers will be full of it. We've got to give the Protestants something. Write us a series of articles on the Orange Order.'

I had picked the same time to come back as had Paddy and Stephen. Paddy had moved to Spain and Stephen had gone back to Canada. I had been part of an exodus, not just a lonely frightened boy, and now, like the others, I was coming back to see if I had been right to leave. Well, none of us had got shot after all, not those who left or those who had stayed — not yet.

I got a couple of months' work on the paper, then a few months more in the BBC and then I left again for another couple of years. I came back again in 1983.

I felt it like a physical blow when I heard that Jim had been shot. I was in my bedsit in Belfast. It was the radio news top story. There was no point in going to see him if he was unconscious in an intensive-care ward. In the following days, his own paper and his media colleagues celebrated his courage and their relief that he was pulling through. They celebrated him as a champion of truth, as if that were the only heroic category they could put him in, yet his love of the story was more to do with its appeal — with the fun he got out of writing it, the mischief — than with its factual grounding or its larger context. I was not part of this celebration of his courage and his genius because I was not part of the media at that time.

But I had seen him just a few weeks before. I had taken a walk towards the mountain and he was on the street with his dog, a red setter, looking relaxed and prosperous and at home. How was I doing? Well, the truth was — and I wasn't going to tell it to Jim — that I had come back after years abroad, knew few people and had no work. 'I'm writing,' I said. I'm sure he knew what that meant.

Jim and I had not been friends. Friendship wouldn't describe the turbulent emotional intensity of our work together as journalists in Belfast ten years earlier. I don't know what would. I was an unformed adult then; he was my news editor and an older and more competent journalist, a temperamental, often angry, ill-formed man himself — fascinating but the worst possible mentor. And this in the middle of a civil war that I had no grasp on and trusted that he, at least, understood better than I did.

What is the truth? It is that I was a child trying to be a man and I had picked another child to follow until, after all the yelling and drinking, I decided I was better away, away from war, away from Jim and away too from the tempestuous family whose ways I had brought into the office with me.

A couple of years later still, when I had picked up the threads of journalism again, I went to East Belfast to interview Andy Tyrie, the head of the loyalist street army, the Ulster Defence Association. Tyrie was an affable man, strangely civil and even jovial, among the thickset bodybuilders with tattoos who hung around him. While we were in his office, one of his senior men, Tommy Lyttle, came in and saw me. We had never met before but my appearance inspired a joke. Lyttle drew out a large brass penknife and opened it. It was sculpted with a sharp point, for violence, not for sharpening pencils. He brought the knife up to my face, grinning, to the corner of my mouth. He said: 'You know, with the wee bit off your beard there and the wee bit off there, you would look just like Jim Campbell.'

I said, 'I worked with Jim.'

He said, 'Every so often, I drive past his house, beep the horn and give him a wee wave — just to scare the shite out of him.'

Tells you everything, doesn't it?

They had enjoyed their war.

# Index